America's
Lost
Generation

AMERICA'S LOST GENERATION

Cameron Lee Cowan

Printed in the United States of America
First Printing: 2025

ISBN: 978-1-954102-26-2 (paperback)
ISBN: 978-1-954102-27-9 (ebook)
Library of Congress Control Number: 2025941368

Edited by Karla Armbuster, Beth Rule
Cover design by Veronica Coello & Jennifer Thomas
Interior design by Amit Dey

Published by:
SOMETHING OR OTHER PUBLISHING LLC
Brooklyn, Wisconsin 53521
For general inquiries: Info@SOOPLLC.com
For bulk orders: Orders@SOOPLLC.com

Other Works by Cameron Lee Cowan

BOOKS

What the Hell Is Going On? A Primer to Understanding Our World in the Age of Trump (2019)

Cast Iron: A Novel (2020)

An unfinished coloring book (2020)

JOURNALISM

Brainz magazine, Senior Contributor

The Cameron Journal (cameronjournal.com), Creative Director

SOCIAL MEDIA

The Cameron Journal podcast (everywhere you listen to podcasts an on video on Spotify and Youtube)

@cameroncowan (X/Twitter, Instagram)

Cameron Lee Cowan (LinkedIn)

@cameronjournal (Tik Tok, Bluesky)

CONTENTS

INTRODUCTION

This book started as I began to analyze what had gone wrong in my life. Most importantly, I was hearing many of my own thoughts in the mouths of others. They reported feeling similarly, "I'm smart, talented, and educated...why am I working at Starbucks?"

When I discovered the Lost Generation subreddit on Reddit, I found a community of people who saw the same things, had similar experiences to mine, and were asking the same question: I did everything I was supposed to do. Why am I broke?

This book is here to tell the story of millennials who survived the Great Recession, also known as the Great Financial Crisis (December 2007 to June 2009), and how they have done it. I collected stories primarily on the r/lostgeneration subreddit on Reddit, then went around the internet and collected the best journalism I could find about people my age who are in their early 30s and looking for solutions and hope—wondering where it all went wrong. It has been more than a decade of grinding struggle. Even for those who reported some actual success, their fears and efforts were just as strong as those who never left the great train station of life.

I wanted to tell their stories and my own. It is time that millennials stood up and told what we have been through and how society has done everything but help us in our time of need. In my research, I found another country and another group of people who had already lived through this experience. Their situation is equally dire. I had been reading the Lost Generation subreddit for some time when I discovered what happened after the 1991 Japanese real estate crisis and the resulting recession.

In 1991, the Japanese housing market collapsed, sending real estate prices across the island nation plunging. Employment skyrocketed in a country where having a job for life was a routine affair after the rebuilding efforts after World War II. That system that moved graduates from school and smoothly into the workforce broke, and it has never recovered.

The 1990s were described as a lost decade for the country as the Japanese economy stubbornly resisted growth despite the best attempts of successive Japanese governments and the Bank of Japan. Japan's national debt grew past its GDP and now stands at 121% of GDP (2022).

Many young Japanese in the early 90s and since have entered a world where the expectation was to have a job for life, and not being recruited out of school could be a career death sentence. The Japanese employment model also meshed with a conformist social attitude that prized group acceptance and conformity above all other concerns. The resulting economic situation has caused unemployment, made it necessary for many young people to remain in their parents' home, and created the unique Japanese phenomena of *hikikomori*, or young men who never leave their childhood homes and sometimes not even their rooms.

The Japanese experience is a cautionary tale. As the United States faces an economic future similar to Japan's, with low growth, high debt, and low demand leading to chronic unemployment, the U.S. can avoid some of the problems facing Japan. However, we should not be too hopeful. If the response to millennials' complaints has been any indication, the U.S. will do little to avoid "Japanization."

When I discovered that young Japanese in 1991 had gone through what has happened to millennials, at least economically, I wanted to know more. I dove into research, looked at online articles, and discovered the work of Michael Zielenziger. His book *Shutting Out the Sun* was invaluable in helping me understand Japanese culture, how punishing it can be on young people, and how little has changed since the economic dynamo of Japan seemed to fail.

To my knowledge, this story has not been told, with personal anecdotes, in any central source with a comprehensive perspective on all the problems facing millennials. From the moment millennials took their first tentative steps into the world, society has constantly criticized millennials for going to college or not going to college and choosing the right degree or not choosing the right degree. Articles have lamented the rate at which millennials aren't getting paid fairly for their work and are stuck in unpaid internships early in their careers. As the years progressed, complaints have abounded about millennials not buying houses, spending too much on rent, demanding student loan relief, and not making the best personal finance decisions. Social media comment sections have been filled with people who don't think millennials have it together and are complaining too much.

However, seeing what happened to an entire generation in Japan was interesting. What to do with them has also been a topic in Japan, especially with the impending retirement crisis of workers who never recovered from the 1991 recession. Japan's pension system is threatened with collapse. The government has tried successive programs to retrain these workers and get them better-paying jobs. Reading their experiences, I found many familiar notes. Seeing as they had experienced the same phenomena seventeen years before the 2008 crisis in the United States, I thought it would be a helpful guide. Unfortunately, from most indications, Japan's lost generation never did recover. It paints a bleak picture for most millennials.

Telling the real experiences of individuals is an integral part of my work. Throughout the book, I begin and end sections with submissions from real Reddit users who wrote their stories to me as a part of this project. It is their tales that inspired me to write this book. Their stories drove me to dig deeper into their situations, their numbers, and more. These people come from a variety of backgrounds. Some are doing alright, while others are not doing well. I have done only basic editing on their words and indicated where I have done so. Otherwise, their words are unvarnished as they were given to me. I included these narratives to show that I'm not the only one who has gone through a hard time. I also show that no matter how well people might have started, life has been difficult for millennials.

In this book, I have tried to take a complete view and picture of millennials and the challenges that we have faced in a world that is very different from the one we were promised. There are stories, as submitted and unedited, from various Redditors who inspired this book, and their stories add a patina of reality to the cold numbers and data. Between the stories and the research, we see how millennials are, as podcaster, NYU professor and author Scott Galloway puts it, "the unluckiest generation."

SECTION I:

AMERICA'S LARGEST GENERATION

A submission from Reddit:

Hello! I saw your post on r/lostgeneration and wanted to know how we could try to contribute to your book. I'm not sure my husband and I qualify because we're doing "just fine" from a boomer's perspective. My husband and I are 35 years old and have been fighting an uphill battle with student debt/trying to live the American Dream for over ten years. We have 160K of student loan debt that resulted from accrued interest on undergraduate loans. We're just now getting to a point where we can make more than minimum payments on the debts, and I know we're fortunate. I talked to my husband earlier today, and we were reflecting on what the past decade has done to us psychologically. If this sounds interesting, I can write up something better. I'm just not sure if you want to hear from people who are "winning" but have still lost more than we'd ever thought possible from a human perspective. Our success is pure luck in many respects, and it's tenuous. I was in pre-med at a solid-state school. With my parent's encouragement, I took a long time to figure out what I wanted to do—ended up with a minor in microbiology and a BA in English when I graduated in 2008. Years later, my employer paid for me to complete an MS in Technical Communication. I'm working on yet ANOTHER employer-funded MS in Computer Science. My career field has changed accordingly. My husband also graduated in 2008 with two degrees, a BS in Chemistry and a BS in Applied Math. He's finally going back for an employer-funded MS in Applied Math from a very good school.

At our lowest point, in 2010, I was pregnant with our daughter. I had to quit my call center job because of pregnancy-related issues. He continued working there. We had no furniture in our apartment because my mom had taken back the furniture she gave me when we moved. He ended up painting fences and doing other odd jobs to make money. He jumped from temp job to temp job, never being hired full-time. We weren't able to pay on the student loans, so we were in default. Both of our parents were disgusted with us and basically blamed us for being in that situation. Ironically, it was my parents who advised us to take on the student debt, to begin with, and get married young because they disagreed with us living together. We're from conservative backgrounds, so we trusted their judgment at the time. (My political leanings have completely flipped since then.)

At the lowest point, I would subconsciously find myself grinding my teeth while I was awake because of the stress from the finances. This whole thing has made me hate the current system, even though we're now winning. I can't get the years back with our kids or undo the damage to the relationships with our family members.

My husband struggled with depression. Our marriage almost dissolved because the stress from the money/family side of things drove him to try to self-medicate. A low point was when he got angry at me for buying a bag of Cheetos with the 5-dollar footlong sub from Subway. It would be easy to think he's an asshole, but we didn't have the money for it. I get where he was coming from. I had anxiety so badly that I thought I had ADHD. I couldn't focus, and it was affecting my work. When we were finally able to pay our bills, my anxiety and the accompanying symptoms "magically" reversed themselves. We haven't been able to give our two daughters the lives we would have wanted for them. We moved to California (not our current state) so that I could take a high-paying job. My husband had just lost yet another chemistry contract, and we were about to be evicted. To do the job, I was gone on travel for business three months out of the year. It was horrifically stressful on my husband and kids. They were 3 and 5 respectively.

The move to California was a positive because it allowed my husband to change careers to software development. Chemistry is largely a dead field in the U.S. due to shipping jobs overseas. Even today, my kids are always asking me why we can't spend more time with them. Why we can't afford to put them in dance class/karate/etc. My oldest daughter has mild to moderate autism, and a lot of our money during the first 7 years of her life went to ABA therapy. That also was what tied me to the job that required me to travel constantly. They were the only ones with insurance that would cover her therapies. We are doing our best to pay for our kids' college so they are never in this position. I'm afraid they'll look back and think we only cared about money. I was always worried we'd end up homeless due to the student debt, as that nearly happened several times when they were very young. The biggest eye-opener for someone coming from a more conservative background is just how little community support there is when you make this kind of mistake. We've lived all over the country following jobs. We've settled in Colorado and finally were able to buy a house last year. It still seems surreal when I see our kids playing in an actual backyard.

As for lingering mental health issues... I'm basically completely paranoid about ever being in that kind of position again. It's almost an obsession that I have to walk myself off of. I never feel secure. My husband is the same way. We never cared about money until we fucked up so badly. I know we're lucky, and I want better for others in our generation and our kids. The current system is broken. Nobody should have to do what we did just to have something approaching a middle-class life. I own my mistakes. We took on debt. We got married young. We had kids young. I know people who didn't make all these mistakes and are worse off. At a certain point, the system is the biggest problem.

CHAPTER 1:

HOW DID WE GET HERE?

A submission from Reddit:

> Mid-30s F(female) STEM Ph.D. here who "did everything right," yet I still feel like I'm stuck in a hopeless, rigged game where I will have to work for evil corporation after evil corporation enriching greedy boomers till I die, just to live semi-comfortably and be able to support myself. My dreams of having a family and/or being able to afford a simple home seem impossible, and instead, I feel like I should just feel lucky that I don't have five roommates or have to live out of a vehicle.

> Unlike people in prior generations, I feel like there are no feasibly-achievable life milestones to look forward to anymore (i.e., home ownership, having children, big vacation/time off, retiring), hence the aptly coined "Millennial Burnout." I did the math, and unless I encounter some kind of cash windfall, I'll just be financially treading water for the rest of my life. I save money and live frugally, but with most decent-paying jobs that are good for my career in expensive, high-income-tax locales, there's really no way I can keep up

with the cost of living and get on the real-estate ladder. I frequently think about how my dad bought multiple houses and comfortably supported a family of 4 with a job that required less education and effort, and then I'm left dumbfounded at how Boomers can point to us and call us the "lazy, entitled" ones.

I know my situation is still better than most, so I feel like I shouldn't complain. But that's precisely why I decided to post. Even as a millennial who has "done well" by millennial standards, I'm left feeling overworked, underpaid, and like life is nothing but a long slog of endless work with little reward.

In 1921, Gertrude Stein had a problem with her car, and she took it to the mechanic for repair. Frustrated with a lack of a good repair by her chosen mechanic, a young man back from World War I who failed to fix her car, she declared, "You are all part of a lost generation." Hemingway would later put this remark in the epigraph for his 1926 book *The Sun Also Rises*. It seemed an apt way to describe those who had come of age during World War I. While the 1920s raged around them and America became its own economic force and a rising global superpower to compete with the old-world empires of Europe, the young people of the 1920s seemed utterly incapable of finding their place in the world. Kate O'Connor, author of an article titled "Lost Generation" published by the University of Oxford wrote, "This accusation referred to the lack of purpose or drive resulting from the horrific disillusionment felt by those who grew up and lived through the war, and were then in their twenties and thirties. Having seen pointless death on such a huge scale, many lost faiths in traditional values like courage, patriotism, and masculinity. Some in turn became aimless, reckless, and focused on material wealth, unable to believe in abstract ideals." The war was over, and while America rushed forward into the twentieth century, it left its young people behind.

After World War II, America focused on putting its discharged soldiers to work or in education. A concerted effort was made to build America into an even larger powerhouse, and young men returning from war were at the center of that project. The returning men and their desire to settle down resulted in a baby boom as these men got married and produced the largest generation in U.S. history. The "Greatest Generation" (a term coined by Dan Rather) gave their children everything they never had in the Depression. Schools were funded, higher education was inexpensive or free, and much of the boomer cohort graduated into a thriving economy with plentiful jobs that often required nothing beyond high school, at least in terms of education.

The boomers and the next cohort, Gen X, would go on to create more children and that resulted in a generation larger than either the Baby Boomers or Gen X. Millennials, born between 1980 and 1995, would exceed their parents in number and grow up in a very different society from the one their parents had known. Unlike the Greatest Generation, the boomers did not give their children the same opportunities that were given to them. Despite this, millennials are the most educated generation in U.S. history. Thirty percent of millennials went to college believing it was the pathway to a better life. Due to the financial management of boomers at all levels of society, the center cohort of millennials would graduate into the worst economy since the Great Depression and be subject to years of austerity. On top of that, they would be burdened with student loan debt that could never be discharged. Even millennials who didn't go to college would be subject to working service industry jobs for low wages that would halt their ability to advance their lives.

In 2008, the American housing market, which had been a source of economic expansion and prosperity since the 1990s and the subsequent dot-com collapse of the early years of the twenty-first century, collapsed under the weight of its debt. American banks had leveraged themselves so much that when the price of housing, which hadn't gone down in decades, finally did, the banking system was brought to its knees. Billions in taxpayer bailouts followed to save the banks, the auto industry, the airlines, and other businesses. No bailout came for regular people, and no bailouts came for the millions of young people born between 1986 and 1991 who had the unfortunate luck to graduate from high school and college during the Great Recession and the long, slow recovery that came after. For those in their early 20s during the Great Recession, there has been little recovery. This book is about these people.

Millennials have struggled to find their place in a world that left them behind and then blamed them for it. In the years after the Recession, the media couldn't publish articles fast enough proclaiming that millennials were killing "industries" ranging from napkins to casual dining restaurants. When millennials sent out hundreds of resumes and got no reply, older people on social media declared that millennials were too lazy, earned the wrong degree, or simply weren't trying hard enough to get a job.

The Great Recession sped up several major economic changes already on the horizon. In 2009, when I was 21 years old, I remember a scrap of an article asking, "What will companies do when they realize they can live without all the clerks and secretaries they have employed?" Companies learned that they could do much more with far fewer people. Entry-level jobs across the economy were eliminated. Even in law firms, clients no longer wanted to pay for a lawyer fresh out of law school to learn the ropes of being a lawyer. Pressure to lower rates forced even large firms to cut staff and hire fewer graduates. Even now, the legal field is saturated with new lawyers. Once seen as a safe profession, the conventional wisdom now is that if you don't attend an elite law school, there's almost no point in going to law school.

College has also suffered from the same conventional wisdom. As Professor Scott Galloway has said over and over again on the popular Pivot podcast with Kara Swisher, elite schools offer an opportunity for ordinary people to do extraordinary things. The millennial who received a liberal arts degree from an unremarkable institution was blamed for not getting into a better school and getting a useful degree. Gen Z has figured out that a college degree is not enough if you want to advance. It has to be in the right field and from a recognizable school. For those of us who went to the second-tier school for a humanities degree, the message from society has been, "Sorry, your help is not wanted."

Although I started researching this book before the outbreak of COVID-19, COVID-19 has only made the situation worse, especially on the inflation side. During the pandemic, we had deflationary pressures (insufficient money was moving). As the pandemic eased, the price of everything seemed to skyrocket, shortages were common, and inflation became a valid concern. This was also combined with high savings rates and less household debt. The pandemic has been the double-whammy millennials collectively feared. Much like how the Asian Financial Crisis was devastating to young Japanese of the 1990s, COVID-19 sent struggling millennials, this time in their late 20s and early 30s (up to 40), back to live with their parents, , and destroyed millions of service sector jobs that had been the financial bread-and-butter of millennials over the past decade.

One quote from my research that stood out to me came from a book called *The Theft of a Decade*, which ends as follows, "The worst boomer theft of all would be to deny us an opportunity to solve our own problems." What are those problems? How did we get here? How do we avoid the fate of the Japanese? How did society change so quickly and so abruptly? How do millennials make a life for themselves that might include the elusive house and children? Those are the questions we're going to explore together.

CHAPTER 2:

WHO ARE MILLENNIALS?

A submission from Reddit:

> When I graduated from college in 2015, I sent out applications and did interviews for months. Eventually, I went broke and started delivering sandwiches to the same offices where I had tried to get a job. I lived in a state capital at the time and had a degree in economics and public administration. But ironically, I couldn't even get an internship. It was a difficult period of my life, and it made me bitter for a while. Luckily, I was able to regroup, financially and emotionally, and get on a different professional path. But I had to totally sacrifice my 20s to the god of money to get it done. I don't have a single friend left. All I care about is working because I'm so scared of being broke again.

Another submission from Reddit:

> Graduated in 2012. Could only get hired as a temp, making 12 bucks an hour. I was lucky enough to move into a

full-time role and changed jobs a few times within the firm to make about 45k salary.

Then, I took a big leap of faith and joined a big company. Moved away from my family and got a big raise. I did well, excelled, created millions of dollars in value for big company. I got good raises and am now at about 75k.

The problem is I'm still well below market value and even below my peers. I've never been paid fairly in my career regardless of experience or value I bring. Now with COVID, prospects in my field are slim.

I'm hitting a wall where it's impossible for me to grow my career while being underpaid for what I do. Hasn't stopped my firm from hiring others for my job at a higher rate. I've been formally acknowledged as the best in my company (in) my field too.

I'm one of the lucky ones and I'm still fucked.

GENERATIONS

Before we dive into the conditions in which America created this lost generation, let's clarify who millennials are and how old they are. Many people think that millennials are those born after the year 2000. A generation refers not only to when you were born but, more importantly, when you came of age. The baby boomers were born between 1945 and 1964 and came of age as early as the early 1960s and as late as the mid-1980s.

Millennials were born between 1980 and 1995. Some researchers note a micro-generation between Generation X, which ended in 1977-79, and more traditional millennials born after 1985. The Xennials, or those born between 1978 and 1985, are a tiny group of people that are also called the "Oregon Trail Generation" because they were the first to play the DOS-based multiple-choice computer game.

These people share some of the experiences of being raised in the 1980s but are also digital natives like their younger counterparts. The Xennials also escaped the worst of the Great Recession because they were out of college before 2008 and had a foothold in the workforce. This advantage would not wholly save them from the layoffs and employment freezes of the Great Recession, but those few extra years of working have left them in a better position than those born after 1985. Millennials had mostly boomer parents, with some first-cohort Gen X parents. There are also late cohort millennials with boomer grandparents.

Millennials are very much a bridge generation, as we will find out. Much has changed during the lifetime of millennials. Economic, technological, and social changes have abounded. In this group, people have lived through a recession, a pandemic, the September 11 attacks, and all the attendant social upheaval that brings. This generation has grown up in a world where being gay was taboo and being LGBT is far more common than it was in the past. The earliest part of the cohort knew of the AIDS epidemic and its associated social changes. The last forty years have been significant, and it has not been easy for young people on any account. It is hard to forge a path forward in a constantly changing world.

The focus of this book is on those born between 1986 and 1991. These millennials were in high school and college right as the Great Recession gutted the American economy. This also means that millennials are now approaching middle age. The oldest millennials turned 40 in 2020. This conversation is not about lazy, entitled college students anymore. This is about people with children to raise, rent to pay, and regular adult bills.

Millennials are curious because they came of age during significant societal transformations and the American economy. They were in high school and college when social media arrived. They tended not to drink or do drugs as much as their older cousins. They were raised strongly about environmentalism, responsibility, staying in school, and success. They were also raised during a great expansion of the American economy and with unprecedented prosperity.

Millennials were the first generation of workers to enter the workforce under truly globalized economic conditions. They had to compete with workers from all over the world. While this certainly affected Gen X and the late cohort of boomers, they also arrived in the workforce after the power of unions had been soundly defeated, beginning with Reagan and his breaking the strike of the Air Traffic Controller's Union and leading into the right-to-work movement of the 1990s and the aughts. This meant that millennials arrived in the workforce with contract work, unpaid internships, and jobs with no benefits being a relatively standard aspect of their working life. This contrasts with their parents, who had robust wages, pensions (sometimes), and higher unionization rates. Their working life has always been a precarious combination of at-will employment with little social safety net, adversely affecting those at the bottom more than those in the middle or the top of wealth and income distribution.

Consequently, millennials have had to make some tough decisions in their lives. Some of the sacrifices might seem trite and small, like not buying napkins and fabric softener, but many of the sacrifices are also far larger, including not being able to buy a home, have children, or have the peace of mind of stable income. They have been balancing childcare costs (for those who had children) and student loan payments on loans accruing interest at eight percent. The millennial story is also about social class, and no discussion of America's lost generation would be complete without breaking down the situation by class.

RACE AND CLASS

A submission from Reddit:

> 31F: My dad moved to the U.S. as a legal immigrant in 1998, then brought my two younger siblings and me here to get

a better education than we would've in the old country. He worked 2-3 jobs to make ends meet while also studying for a degree in civil engineering (he got his degree in early 2008 and was immediately hired for a really well-paying job, only to be laid off right before Christmas due to the 2008 economic downturn. He's never been able to recover from that and has had to work minimum-wage jobs ever since). As a result, we barely saw him, and when we did, he was usually in a stinky mood because he was always so exhausted. And despite all of his efforts, he had his car repo'ed four or more times, and almost every fall/winter, we'd have our gas shut off since he couldn't always afford to pay the bill on time. Imagine being in the top floor apartment of a 3-story unit without heat in the middle of a northeastern U.S. winter! We'd have to heat up water in the stove if we wanted a warm shower. My siblings and I worked hard to learn the language, assimilate, and get good grades, while missing our mom, relatives, and childhood friends like crazy.

I started 10th grade in the U.S. and excelled in school. As the oldest, I also had an after-school job to help my dad with bills. My teachers saw that I had real potential, especially in math and science, so they encouraged me to apply to the computer engineering program at a private, prestigious, and crazy expensive university. My dad, not having grown up in the U.S., didn't know anything about the college application process or how I was going to pay for it, so I had to figure it all out on my own. I managed to get into said prestigious university, scored a couple scholarships, but still had a $40k/year gap that needed to be covered by student loans. Again, being relatively new to the country and all we didn't understand how this all worked so I naively took on those loans. Well, I got to college and immediately realized that I was at a huge disadvantage. The majority of the student body was insanely wealthy and had been preparing for college their entire lives.

During our very first computer engineering intro class, I knew I was screwed. The teacher asked some questions to get a feel for where everyone was, and, besides me, literally, everyone else in the lecture hall spoke fluent computer engineering, so the teacher announced to the class that he was going to skip the basics and get right to the meat of things. I floundered for an entire semester and eventually went to my college counselor, who helped me switch to civil engineering, which was supposed to be more manageable. Nope. After two more semesters of pure misery, of not having money to eat despite being on the school's dining plan, of not being able to afford to go home during spring break while everyone else was off partying for the week, of not having the money to buy proper shoes and clothes for the brutal upstate NY winters, of not being able to afford the expensive textbooks that had to be bought brand-new every semester and, thus, not completing my school work and falling behind, I had to switch to an "easier" degree.

So I went into hospitality management, and well, that shit degree hasn't gotten me anything other than a gigantic boulder of a student loan debt that I've defaulted on multiple times since hospitality jobs don't pay well, totally damaging my credit. Because of my bad credit, I can't qualify for a mortgage or any other type of loan. I live in an apartment complex where rent has gone up by at least $100/month every year since I moved here four years ago, which is a lot, even though I have a roommate. It's now at just shy of $1,700/month but I can't afford to move out to a cheaper place (yep, you read that correctly). Because of my bad credit, I'd be required to pay a security deposit as well as first and last month's rent, not to mention application fees and moving costs. Last April, I finally scored a job that paid just shy of $50k/year, which was huge for me. I don't have any kids, so that amount of money, coupled with my frugal lifestyle, would go a long way.

I was finally able to start paying off my debts and get on track with cleaning up my credit. Fast forward to early March (2020) of this year when my company decided to eliminate my position due to the pandemic, leaving me high and dry. They managed to find new positions within the company for the other two girls that worked the same position as me, but I was let go despite having recently had an excellent performance review and great rapport with everyone in the office. Well, now I'm back to square zero with no idea when I'll be able to get another job because of our current situation. I've got a college degree, speak five languages fluently, have excellent work ethic, can do just about anything that's thrown my way without complaining, have an easy to get along with demeanor, and yet I don't qualify for most high-paying jobs even if my resume matches the job description. So much for the American dream and pulling yourself up by your bootstraps.

One of the issues I ran into in working on this book was quantifying two seemingly disparate stories and outcomes. When I read submissions like the ones I have printed in this book, it is easy to see how millennials have been given a short shrift in life opportunities. However, there are many millennials who have no such problems. I told someone about this book, and they said, "I have four millennial children, and I don't know about anything you're talking about." Luckily, they are not affected by many of the factors that follow in this book. I realized between looking at the data and listening to people that class structure and hierarchy have a deleterious effect on millennial progress.

I can split the situation into a few groups that I have identified:

1. Upper-class millennials who are surprised by downward mobility

2. College-educated millennials but not working in their field.

3. College-educated and working in their field for low pay

4. College dropouts/high school graduates who are surprised by the lack of upward mobility.

It should be noted that while millennials are the most educated generation in U.S. history, two-thirds of millennials did not go to college. The picture has been equally bleak for these young people. Each of these groups has a disparate but connected set of problems.

The story has been very different for millennials from economic privilege who could afford to take an unpaid internship, move home with parents, change careers, or get help buying a home. Many of those who made it out did not understand the experience of the rest of us. A coach told me that his friend moved to New York City for a finance job and got laid off soon after because of the Great Financial Crisis. He spent a year and a half unemployed and then was fine. He was lucky, but there was no word on how he survived during his unemployment. For those upper-class millennials who had family help to smooth over a job loss or false career start, they were likely able to get back on the ladder and continue on with life. However, for those in the middle class and below who did not have access to family resources, or in the case of minority and immigrant groups who needed to help their families, the situation that those millennials have had to endure is more complicated.

The recession hurt the aspirational working class and lower middle class kids the most. Why? They needed those entry-level jobs fresh out of college the most. Some could not return home to their parents or get help. They had to take whatever job they could get and hope they could afford to live. They were shunted into the low-paying service-sector jobs that abounded post-2008. Those stories are in this book, too. There were also other ways in which millennials who aspired to social mobility were disadvantaged.

The massive gap in understanding the workforce and college is a factor that isn't often studied but has outsized effects on those who are the first in their family to go to college. The problem doesn't stop there either; after college, millennials with connections to the job market left their peers behind. Unlike in years past, it is hard to start a career when you know no one connected to that career. I learned the hard way how important it was to develop a network and use those connections for job opportunities. Creating these networks is even more complicated for people of color due to discrimination and bias. Combine that with coming from a working-class background and needing to work after classes in college. You can get a great education and have no foot in the door to any sort of career. I will explore this further when we discuss entry-level jobs and the catch-22 of needing experience, as it's difficult to get hired unless you have experience. This hiring dynamic is combined with a hollowing out of the entry-level job market following the 2008 recession as well.

The result is that the people who have suffered adversely in the economy are trying to maintain their middle-class status or move into the middle class. The economic gains have been so unevenly distributed that the real story of the post-Great Financial Crisis period is how the middle class, especially the lower middle class and working class, have been impacted by these economic changes and how people have been economically left behind.

Millennials are also the most diverse generation in U.S. history, with nearly fifty percent of millennials being BIPOC (black, indigenous, people of color). America's new racial diversity has been felt across the culture wars as our country has engaged in new conversations on race, police brutality, and structural racism. The rise of the "social justice warrior" (SJW) or "woke" person started with millennials back in 2011-2013. New social attitudes emerged that caused a cascading set of social changes that have rocked the country to its core. Social change ramped up and was further amplified by the George Floyd protests of 2020 and the many Black Lives Matter protests that would follow.

Popular protests have been happening since the Great Financial Crisis, but the conversation on race has not been as charged since 1968. Millennials and Gen Z have grown up in a more diverse world than their parents. By 2050, the United States will no longer be majority "white" (European-descended). This shift will be felt primarily by millennials and now Gen Z. Interracial relationships, while not terribly common, are more acceptable now than ever before. These changes are all credited to the fact that the picture of the country has changed. Millennials helped put Barack Obama into the White House in 2008, a watershed moment for the nation. As I have written elsewhere, America is trying to find out if it can still be a country with more than one voice at the table, and it will be millennials who will lead the charge and make the decisions that will answer that question. If diversity is our strength, then it will be up to millennials to make that a reality. The question remains: will older generations let us do it?

ENTITLED AND LAZY

No two words about millennials have been thrown around more than entitled and lazy. Pundits like Simon Sinek and many others have complained that millennials want everything—they want it right now and don't want to work for it. Most publications spent most of the late aughts and 2010s complaining about this. Much digital ink has been spilled about what is wrong with millennials and why they can't get it together. Most comments boil down to the old canard: Millennials are entitled and lazy.

America's largest and most educated generation seemed unwilling to work to build a successful life. However, the situation is far more complicated than that.

Annie Lowry, a reporter for *The Atlantic*, tweeted on Twitter (now X) this prescient post in the summer of 2020:

> The millennials entered the workforce during the worst downturn since the Great Depression. Saddled with debt, unable to accumulate wealth, and stuck in low-benefit, dead-end jobs, they never gained the financial security that their parents, grandparents, or even older siblings enjoyed. They are now entering their peak earning years in the midst of an economic cataclysm more severe than the Great Recession, near guaranteeing that they will be the first generation in modern American history to end up poorer than their parents. Compounding their troubles, millennials are, for now, disproportionate holders of the kind of positions disappearing the fastest: bartenders, half of restaurant workers, and a large share of retail workers. For the most part, kids of the 1980s and 1990s did it right: They avoided drugs and alcohol as adolescents. They went to college in record numbers. They sought stable, meaningful jobs and stable, meaningful careers. A lot of good that did.

It seemed like this wasn't a mere career problem either; it extended into dating. Why get to know someone when you could just swipe? Simon Sinek in his viral video on millennials pointed out that it is nearly impossible to build a relationship when millennials don't have any sense of delayed gratification. Are we so broken?

These attitudes about millennials have persisted, too. Erstwhile demographic researcher and public intellectual Peter Zeihan tweeted in 2022: "One of 1000 ways the #Millennials are no longer the cool kids. The generation after them - #GenZ- is smarter, harder-working, more competitive, more responsible, and neurotic messes like their parents." He commented on an article from the Telegraph about how millennials aren't traveling as much, which would have ramifications in the travel industry. We can't win, can we?

Millennials have struggled with perception. I've had too many people on social media and even in person complain about everything wrong with millennials. Even as Gen Z has burst onto the scene, people still complain about millennials. We can't seem to get a win. Any speech about demographics causes an eye roll when millennials are brought up.

So why do people perceive millennials as lazy and entitled? How can the most educated generation in American history who didn't drink or do drugs nearly as much as their boomer parents or their Gen X cousins be entitled and lazy? Again, this is a perception issue. Older people felt like millennials showed up to the workplace ready to work but already wanted to be in charge and advance quickly through the ranks rather than spend years grinding away. Of course, this supposes they could get those entry-level positions (more on that later). Others were stuck in service and retail roles, which also garnered critique that millennials simply weren't working hard enough to get good jobs. There was never a discussion about the fact that those good jobs simply didn't exist anymore.

The other problem with the idea that "if you work hard, you will succeed" is that it can be hard to see any reward for working hard. Given the stagnation of wages and the rise of inflation in the post-pandemic period, many folks have expressed online (and to me personally) that the reward isn't the same as it once was for their parents. I have friends who work, make good money, and do not own their own homes. They pay high rents to live in various apartments. These economic conditions worsen for those who live in major cities where most job creation has occurred over the past decade. The consensus advice has always been the same: "don't get a useless degree," or "learn to code," or even "go into the trades." There is no talk about how to fix the problem (wages and benefits) or find a workaround.

Instead of a productive discussion on the structural issues around employment in this country, the advice is always the same: work harder and figure it out. Those who don't find this course of action compelling are called "entitled and lazy." Apparently, it is entitled and lazy to desire a wage high enough to live like an adult where you can afford to pay all your bills, save money, and improve your life over time. Instead, millennials have been criticized for not jumping at the chance to work a job that pays $15 per hour but still requires a degree.

We live in a country where the minimum wage is no longer a living wage, and even in places where the minimum wage has risen to $15 per hour, it's still not a living wage for many people. That is when another piece of advice is thrown about, "get a better job that pays more." Incidentally, during the Great Resignation of 2021-2022 and the Quiet Quitting movement, people were often doing precisely that. It impacts the service industry as restaurants and others struggled to hire the staff they need.

The conversation has never turned toward what could help Americans—especially millennial Americans—improve their lot. Instead, we have simply chosen to vilify millions of people who are struggling and make it all their fault.

INTERNET AND TECHNOLOGY

Millennials are the last generation to remember life before the internet. They were early adopters of smartphones and social media and were some of the first people to use those devices and services. Many millennials grew up with a computer in their home and were the first kids to have cellphones. Gen Z may be native to the internet, but millennials were the pioneers that have made our current media ecosystem possible.

Millennials are in the uncanny valley, stuck between the old and new worlds. Indeed, the 2008 crisis was the breaking point of the old world of the millennials' youth, and after 2008, nothing was the same. The senior advice didn't work anymore. The old working methods did not fit, and millennials were adrift. The contributions of technology have undoubtedly fueled the feeling of disconnection. Social media has been a force for new connections and new ways of discovering content and content creators, but its effects on mental health are now being understood. Millennials have been on the front lines of the enviable Instagram photos and curated experiences over video and other mediums. The effects on culture, mental health, and even relationships have been profound. As we will find throughout this book, the influence of technology is inextricably linked to the story of millennials.

Now that we understand more about millennials and who they are, we can understand their background and the world millennials grew up in. This is important because major geopolitical events occurred between 1980 and the present day. Two stand out particularly: The fall of the Soviet Union in 1991 and the 9/11 terrorist attacks in 2001. I like to call this period Pax Americana.

CHAPTER 3:

GROWING UP IN PAX AMERICANA

A submission from Reddit:

> If you want another perspective, I'm 32 and skipped college completely and have had a great life. In the middle of high school, I realized that college was just a really expensive culling mechanism and thought it would be better to skip completely. Bet has paid off well. I don't want to distract from the overall message, but pm (private message) me if you'd like. Good luck with the book.

On Christmas Day, 1991, Mikhail Gorbachev announced that the Soviet Union was breaking up. The great nuclear threat from the Cold War was over. Communism had been defeated by market economics, and the world was ready to enjoy permanent peace among its great powers for the first time since before World War II. It had been seventy-seven years of two major world wars and decades of detente between the world's great ideological systems. A world of peace had finally arrived, in time for the celebration of the new millennium coming at the end of the decade.

Economically, things were improving in the United States as well. Bill Clinton would defeat George H.W. Bush in the 1992 presidential election, and he would preside over the most significant expansion of the American economy until that time. Serving as the first boomer president, Bill Clinton built on Nixon's work opening China and grant China the most favored nation trading status within the World Trade Organization. He passed and signed the North American Free Trade Agreement, among other foundational treaties that would create the world of globalization that we know today and was ever-present in pre-pandemic America.

Culturally, the 1990s were a heady time. Racial tensions pock-marked the early years of the decade, with the Rodney King riots breaking out in Los Angeles after the police responsible for beating Mr. King were acquitted of any wrongdoing by a nearly all-white jury. The rise of crack and other street drugs would lead Congress to pass the now-infamous 1994 crime bill that would bring mandatory mini-mums for certain crimes and would ramp up mass incarceration within the United States.

The message to children during this time was straightforward, and millennials would follow it (mostly) to the letter: stay in school, care about other people, care about the state of the planet, don't do drugs, stay out of jail, go to college, and you will do well in life. A quick tour of children's programming of the late 80s and early 90s will show this message repeated over and over again. Shows like Teenage Mutant Ninja Turtles, Captain Planet, Arthur, The Magic School Bus, and others would reinforce this message repeatedly. The message the boomers had been given by their parents was very different but just as insidious.

Unlike the boomers who took the list of "rules" their parents had oppressively shoved onto them and discarded it, millennials adopted the message from their boomer and early Gen X parents and tried to follow it. Gen X was given very little by their parents and expected less. Dubbed the generation that checked out, Gen X has always gone their way with things and is fiercely independent. Boomers rejected the system, Gen X checked out of the system, and millennials tried to win the system.

No conversation about the 1990s would be complete without discussing the rise of technology. The personal computer and its smartphone progeny would figure heavily in the lives of millennials. They were the first generation to be raised with computers in many homes and the last generation to remember a world before everything had become digital. Many millennials are digital natives who know how to use a phone book and a paper map. The rise of technology in every aspect of our lives was just beginning when millennials were children, and by the time most millennials were graduating from college and moving back in with their parents, tech had all but taken over. Millennials were, by and large, ready for this change and have since demanded an ever-increasing digital marketplace. Millennials would rather use an app than make a call. Growing up in digital environments is where many of the youngest members of the generation are most comfortable. Millennials also benefitted from the rise of gaming culture and the rise of the internet. The internet would change our lives, and millennials were the young people at the forefront of these changes. They were the young explorers of a world of websites, chat rooms, chat apps, and blogs. Later, they would forge a new frontier in social media and be a major contributor to social media takeover, cord-cutting, and digitization. Gen X might have invented the tech, but millennials made it cool and famous.

I do not think it to be nostalgic to say that it felt like the world was moving forward and we were making significant progress toward a hopeful future. It felt like things were getting better and that many of the demons our country faced were finally behind us. A particular upward trajectory seemed to be pervasive in the air. Even in the social sphere, the 1990s sported many firsts on the LGBTQIA+ front. People have forgotten that Ellen Degeneres coming out as a lesbian on national television was major news for nearly a month.

This age was also marked by peak consumerism. Shopping was not merely an activity but a hobby, a pursuit. Splashy catalogs and glossy ads flooded mailboxes, showcasing shiny goods to buy. Part of this was due to major credit expansion. The American economy had finally shaken off the malaise of the 1970s and 1980s, and President Bill Clinton presided over unprecedented growth. Alan Greenspan was treated like an economic god because he was able to manage the economy to create prosperous growth without the terrible inflation that had plagued the economy before.

Many people who grew up in these years probably remember it as a magical time. It was not so magical; human memory is faulty this way, but many of the problems that we have now were much less present in the years after the Cold War. Most middle class people owned their own homes; college was far cheaper for Gen X; and "good jobs" were still available. How this system came undone will be discussed in due course.

It was not uncommon to have single-earner households with a stay-at-home parent. However, two working parents were more common, especially as boomer and early cohort Gen X women tried to have it all, an erstwhile subject of popular TV. Productivity was up; technology was enabling people to do more than before. The world was changing, but it seemed more manageable. As the world moved into the new millennium, there was a hope that we could move into a new era of cooperation under the "new world order" of democratic values, economic liberalism, and peace.

Growing up in this time was unique but also insidious. We were preparing for a world and a future that wouldn't exist just a few short years into the new century. It was far too late when we figured out what had gone wrong or that there was a problem. In the background of the fall of the Soviet Union, housing was being commodified, globalization would further undermine developed world economies, and a transfer of wealth from the bottom to the top would hit its stride. It would be trite to say that no one said anything about this. Sadly, the warnings of people like Noam Chomsky did not reach broad appeal. Senator Bernie Sanders was just a weird guy from Vermont to whom attention need not be paid.

Trying to write about the 1990s is like trying to write about an impossible dream. The vibrancy of pop culture, the ability to go into careers that pay from the earliest stage, and the capacity for skills and education to pay off in significant ways make it seem like they are from another planet. It is so foreign to how we live now, where things are much more precarious.

Pax Americana wasn't all roses. There were a variety of violent incidences like Desert Storm, the Oklahoma City bombing, the attack at Waco, Ruby Ridge, and the attacks on American embassies in Kenya and Tanzania that hinted at the troubles that were bubbling underneath. The degradation in wages and wage growth had already gone on for 20 years by the decade's end. Productivity was increasing rapidly, but wages stopped tracking that metric in 1977. Still, the availability of credit card debt, the falling cost of authentic goods, and relatively low interest rates allowed the American consumer to power the global economy and post significant economic gains. It is no secret why younger people, millennials and Gen Z, romanticize the 1990s as much as their parents might romanticize the 1950s or 1960s.

CHAPTER 4:

It's All Our Fault

A submission from Reddit:

> I also think millennials are like 3% to blame for their plot in life, if they finance a useless education, and experience agony for the simple dilemma of being at home for a while. It was the humble pie I needed to eat, but I can't speak for a cohort of what, like 74 mils?
>
> What is NOT millennials fault is staggering obscene ungodly exploitative rent prices, prohibitively expensive travel, the shackles of student debt and debt peonage if you want to better yourself generally, and the outsourcing of jobs by magnitudes that are kind of unspeakable. I think more people should become CNAs though and that for the roughly 1,000 whatever dollars it costs to get the license to do that it will and does pay off handsomely...I've definitely developed what I coined "career Tourette's"—like a neurological compulsion to think about career every second of every day or just overfocus on it anyway—a term I often share with some pride, I think it's kind of neat and to the

point, but yeah…I had the same staggering rude awaken-
ing everyone else did. Upon almost graduating and having
thousands dollars debt and working at a Wendy's full- time
while doing school full-time absolutely busting ass making
like 9k things definitely dawned on me. I have a weird tic
where I do the "wilhelm scream" sound partially ironically
partially not at a very low volume, basically as a tic sometimes because I'm so burnt out. I just let er' rip if I'm at a
low wage job where they need me desperately and it's clear
it doesn't matter.

It would not be hyperbole to say that millennials have been unfairly
blamed for the problems that they face. We've all seen the comment
sections on social media around the same articles complaining about
millennials' decisions. During this height during 2010-2019, the infamous avocado toast and iPhone became easy criticisms of the younger
generation. If young people were serious about improving their financial conditions, they would do without "luxuries" like smartphones,
avocado toast, and coffee. When the future seems uncertain, why not
buy that avocado toast, take that Instagram-worthy trip, and buy that
nice item? Much of the criticism around millennials has been their odd
economic and financial decisions.

In the years after the financial crisis, many older adults complained
that if millennials were so badly off, why were they traveling so much,
eating expensive foods, and buying iPhones? As if mere objects could
solve life's problems like low wages and rising rent costs.

Millennial trauma is different. There are certainly those who have
trauma from war, but despite the 20-year war in Iraq and Afghanistan,
the number of young people who have served is relatively small as
compared to the population. However, the trauma of 2008 and its
resulting non-existent recovery are quite another kind of trauma.

American millennials suffer much of the same malaise. Life is
too expensive and wages are too low. Pass the avocado toast and

the iPhone. The criticism of phones is particularly poignant. The rise of the smartphone put the power of a personal computer into everyone's pockets, and cellphone companies soon found a way to make phones more affordable with monthly leasing plans. A smartphone might be perceived as just another dry status symbol, but it is increasingly an important tool in today's modern world. Many jobs require online applications and email follow-ups before an interview. Socialization takes place online, too, meaning social media apps are an essential way to keep up with friends and social obligations, and managing money and other bills can often be done through an app with paperless billing. This means many millennials usually run their entire lives from their phone. This millennial certainly does. I paid all my monthly bills before working on this part of the book today. Using seven different apps, I updated my Mint budgeting app and paid all my bills in about 15 minutes.

Commentator and social media darling Simon Senek, an outspoken critic of millennials, blames millennials' propensity for instant gratification for their inability to build a career or maintain a relationship. Our world has made it seem like everyone else is living a magical life of travel and sex with attractive people, and with dating apps, it looks like the right person for us should be just a swipe away. A career takes time to build. It requires connections, a proven work history, and plenty of time, as the prime working and earning years don't happen until the ages the millennials are hitting.

Senek has a fair point on the surface, especially for those who like to criticize the under-45 set, but it doesn't reflect the realities millennials have faced, especially in their early working years. What is the point of trying to build a career when a college degree is no guarantee of a prosperous future and building a career requires endless job changes, especially if greater pay is desired? The connections aspect certainly has merit, but what about those from lower socioeconomic backgrounds who might find building those connections difficult? And what about those stuck in jobs where the chance for advancement seems hopeless?

This is partly due to older workers not retiring and companies trimming their labor force to the minimum to save on costs.

The modern hookup culture has indeed characterized millennial dating. Although millennials, despite inventing hookup culture, are having less sex than their parents. There are various reasons why marriage and household formation have been falling for those in their prime working years. For women, forming a household with a partner, especially a man, can be a losing game economically, and this has primarily to do with the dimming job prospects of men, especially uneducated men. Another factor, which is very similar to Japan, is that women are more career-focused than their mothers. In the 1990s, women were told they could have a successful career, a wonderful marriage, and happy children. Looking at popular culture today, that doesn't exist as much. Millennials lived with their mothers, who tried to have it all and lived with the consequences. Much like Gen X before them, they became latchkey kids or shuffled to various schools and daycares with parents who were too busy with work to give them the attention they desired. As it turns out, women couldn't quite have it all, and millennials have made a decisive choice. Women of my generation, especially career-minded women, have often chosen to sacrifice childbearing in favor of career pursuits, and even that is an economic decision.

Much of this decision not to have children comes down to cost. Living on one income isn't sustainable in many areas, so parents need daycare services. According to the Department of Labor, the annual cost of childcare is extreme, "childcare prices range from $4,810 ($5,357 in 2022 dollars) for school-age home-based care in small counties to $15,417 ($17,171 in 2022 dollars) for infant center-based care in very large counties. These prices represent between 8% and 19.3% of median family income per child." That means if someone has two children in a high cost living area, $30,000 could be needed for just childcare. Even in poorer areas, where wages are lower, two children would have parents putting out nearly $10,000 in childcare expenses annually. This is an outsized amount for a modest household income of $55,000. For many families, this means that one parent stays home. I've seen this among my friends. I recall when a long-time friend of mine finally placed her son in preschool and returned to work, she called me and said, "I talked to adults for the first time in four years!" She and her husband worked opposite shifts for years to avoid having to pay for childcare. They saw each other for about two hours per day. They don't plan on having more children.

On top of this burden, children also bring other commitments like being involved at school, various fees for activities, scheduling concerns, and much more for the career-minded woman to consider. Children are a huge expense. Raising a child in America can cost $500K by age 18, and for many women, the motherhood penalty for salaries and promotions is an authentic problem. Even in a loving, stable relationship, the entire household loses money and income from this situation.

Many mothers, especially poorer women, have to give birth and hurry back into the workplace in a society with no maternity or paternity leave, paid or otherwise. My mother was in this very boat as a single Mom. She was lucky to have family child care available but returned to her job dispatching ambulances a week after giving birth (which took three days because I do my own thing).

Unsurprisingly, many millennials either delay having children or choose not to have them. As we will find out, similar calculations are made by our friends in Japan, a country with demographics far worse than those in the United States.

When all the hallmarks of adulthood, home ownership, and family seem out of reach, avocado toast seems like a good option. Doing something today, much like the Japanese with their handbags and other symbols of prosperity, makes more sense than denying themselves any pleasure for nearly no hope of ever achieving the American Dream. Two thousand dollars is hardly a drop in the bucket for buying a home where down payments routinely are tens of thousands of dollars, but thanks to cheap travel (pre-COVID-19), it can be the start of paying for a nice trip to Southeast Asia or even a week in Europe. The Instagram posts are merely a social media bonus.

In an unstable world where the future seems uncertain, which was undoubtedly true in the years after 2008, self-denial today doesn't make any sense. The COVID-19 crisis has proven that the future remains uncertain. It is hard enough to get human beings to plan for the future, but when the world seems doubtful, it is easier to take what you can today because tomorrow is not promised. For millennials, this has been true for their entire working lives.

Life can present all sorts of challenges to people. There are health challenges within a family, job loss, a car breaking down beyond repair, a career change, and bigger things like a house fire or the sudden death of a spouse. In this environment and for this generation of people, we have quickly learned that you can't make a mistake. When it comes to money or any situation in life, you have to be hyper vigilant because you might never recover once you fall. The ladder to stability and success is complex; mistakes or missteps can have catastrophic consequences for years.

One of the comments that I received via Reddit stood out to me:

> We've managed to scrape some semblance of middle class, but it was so fucking tiring. I feel like I've lived a whole lifetime at 30. There was no room for error, I made the right choice numerous times and it was barely, through luck alone, enough. My fate was almost never in my hands, job loss now would still be almost unbearable. It's taken hundreds, maybe thousands, of applications, dozens of interviews to eke out a wage increase more than a pittance each year. Any lapse in vigilance would slowly lead to poverty. The world does not want us to succeed. All the while, someone with capital could have made as much as I have in a decade in a few weeks on the market. People owning yachts and shit because they come from money, while others less fortunate

are basically homeless. We obtained the "American dream" and not only is it nothing special, the guilt of our relative success being a lottery sucks. I spend frivolously because the future is so uncertain, nihilism has been beaten into me. There is no bright-eyed and bushy tailed in my world. We happened to avoid major catastrophes, that's it. If either of us had ever lost our ability to work, or needed major medical care, or any of our parents needed help, we'd not be where we are now, and others our age were not so fortunate.

The experiences of people like this comment define what economist Guy Standing calls the new precariat. In the example from this Redditor, he achieved education as a certified pharmacy technician and, alongside his wife, managed to buy a house with help from his parents. In previous times, two incomes with solid jobs would have made them solidly middle class. Currently, they are scraping by with housemates and have no plans to have children. This is what millennials face today.

Doing well in life is a combination of mistakes, luck, and intelligent decisions. One of the struggles for millennials is that they did indeed try to make all the "right" decisions. Millennials had less sex than boomers or Xers. They committed less crime, too. Teen cigarette smoking plummeted to the single digits. Millennials tried to win the system.

However, millennials also had pressures. Kids who couldn't pay attention in class were often drugged with Ritalin or Adderall. Helicopter parenting became a common phrase for parents who were always around their kids and seemingly overly involved in their lives. The infamous participation awards eased the ego hits of losing at sports or any competition. Millennials also had a greater cultural awareness than previous generations, fueled chiefly by the burgeoning internet and its connections.

The boomers' greatest mistake was simple: a lack of investment in the system that created the Great Prosperity. Instead, boomers extracted everything that they could from a system designed for their success by their parents, who knew what it was like to go without food, water, and money and live in actual deprivation of the Depression and war. The boomers were a generation that voted with self-interest at the first opportunity (Reagan) and have continued to build and create a system to enrich themselves. This is especially true in the upper echelons of society. Instead of creating a future for their children, they were more concerned with their property values.

The world has changed in a short period of time. I think there is a certain lack of understanding of how the world has changed. I, for one, am lucky to have parents who understand how hard it has been and how the world has changed. They respect the hard work I have put in to create something for myself and all my random jobs. Many are not so lucky, and there are plenty of boomers who are unsympathetic to the millennial plight.

So why does it seem so hard to care about the problems of millennials despite them being real human people in our society?

CHAPTER 5:

WHY NO ONE SEEMS TO CARE

A quote found on Facebook:

> My generation was in elementary school when 9/11 happened, which started the longest undeclared war in U.S. history. In the year of my high school graduation the 2008 subprime mortgage bubble burst and crippled the world's economy. Wages have not kept up with inflation or productivity since the 70s, college tuition has gone up over 1000%, the war on drugs is still a thing, our government is a corrupt gaggle of corporatist whores, identity politics is in full swing, the "throw away" life styles of past generations has left a country-sized mass of plastic in the ocean and the climate got skull fucked by humanity's greed. But yeah, we use smart phones (access to the collective knowledge of humanity in your pocket) and eat avocados. Real pieces of shit we are.

One of the great mysteries of our time is how little has been done to solve the problems of younger people. Social media comment sections are usually filled with two groups: those who acknowledge the issue and those who deny its very existence and blame the under-45 folks for simply not working hard enough. One of the tropes that were quite popular over the last decade was the 25-year-olds (usually a couple) who bought a house through "hard work" and "saving money" but had help from mom and dad. People will praise their virtue and say, "See, if they can do it, why can't you?" Without understanding that underneath the surface is family support to make that advancement possible. Their parents didn't need a loan from the Bank of Mom and Dad to buy a house. Social media makes it seem so easy, and frustrated people open their banking app and wonder why they aren't keeping up. This is an area where class has a great effect. For millennials who come from an economic background where they enjoy family resources, much of the impact of our present economic situation has been mitigated. For everyone else, the world has nothing to offer but a new status of precarity.

It remains a mystery to me why there has not been more focus on improving the lot for young workers. Ann Helen Peterson wrote an article for the PBS Newshour titled "Can't Even: How Millennials Became the Burnout Generation." She wrote, "Millennials 'Can't Even' get ahead—they're already too far behind, … Millennials live with the reality that we're going to work forever, die before we pay off our student loans, possibly bankrupt our children with our care, or get wiped out in a global apocalypse. That might sound like hyperbole—but that's the new normal, and the weight of living amidst that sort of emotional, physical, and financial precarity is staggering."

Here is where a dose of reality might be helpful. Human history is filled with tragedy. Most of human history has been "brutish and short." War, disease, famine, and much more have filled the human story across the planet. Humanity has spent most of its development finding ways to control things threatening lives and collective security. From this perspective, being a millennial is pretty good. We don't face the challenges of our forebears. In this way, Scott Galloway is correct. Millennials aren't particularly put-upon, but they are unlucky.

Unfortunately, the world our parents prepared us for no longer exists, so this age is to feel a certain amount of disconnection. It is easy to look outside or on social media and wonder where everything went wrong. Boomers certainly think about the world, but the disconnection feels much different at age 60 than at 30. Disconnection from the world is hard to handle when balancing student loans, deciding whether to have children, and wondering how to make enough money to survive in an unfriendly job market.

The year 2008 ended a large credit expansion, and the austerity policies of the world's governments meant a slow recovery. Like the Japanese after 1991, the economy didn't bounce back and people were left behind. For many millennials, this feeling of being left behind will haunt them their whole lives. The trouble is that when people complain about being left behind, few people want to hear their complaints or even acknowledge a problem. This was also true for the Japanese. As we will find out, the issue of the employment ice age only began to garner government attention when it started to affect the pension system.

There has been no social program to help millennials who needed to retool for a different world than we were promised. There has not been a federal response to prime-age males' lack of labor participation. In my first book, *What the Hell is Going On?*, I wrote an essay on the ten million missing men. It was based on an article in *The Atlantic* about the same subject. My tone was a bit dismissive at the time. However, as the years passed, I realized this problem deserved to be taken seriously. Of those prime-age males (25-55), millennials entirely fall within that age range. When the labor force participation rate is a modest 62 percent (in 2022), it means millions of people are economically marginalized.

This should be the subject of presidential debates, but it did not come up in 2016 or 2020. The only person to address it at some level was Donald Trump. He did an excellent job speaking to the marginalized people who had been economically left behind. Despite the nature of his message, it certainly resonated. He received the most votes in American history in 2016 and the second most in American history in 2020, only bested by Joe Biden, who took the top spot. In 2020, he increased his vote share among every demographic except white men. This trend reversed in 2024 with white men and white women breaking decisively for President Trump. Politically, the lack of help for people, especially men, has political consequences. Much of our current discourse swirls around these problems.

Some people will still complain that millennials are simply too entitled, too selfish, too-anything, and that there is no reason to focus on the problems of millennials. This attitude is another marginalization. Millennials are real people raising kids, buying houses, and trying to afford childcare and retirement. For many, those milestones took many more years than they had planned. They have been through the double punch of a recession and a pandemic. Millennials have had complete economic devastation twice before the age of 50. In our modern era, this will have life-long consequences for most. While millennials might not face famine, disease, and flood like in ages past, in our current capitalistic economic model, an economic downturn is just as bad as the floods and diseases of old. It can be the difference between getting to buy a house or grinding on as a member of the new precariat.

Within the millennial soul, at least for some, there is a certain sense of disappointment and loss. We are living in a future denied. This is when you can do everything right and lose for no reason other than dumb luck and bad timing. History is full of that, too. The poor person who opened a business in 1929 had no idea there wouldn't be a functioning economy shortly afterward. Someone with big plans in 1939 might have turned their whole life upside down by an inconvenient European invasion. I'm sure someone in 1941 had a charming picnic planned for December 7, and it was ruined by the Japanese deciding it was time to bomb Pearl Harbor. Those are just recent examples. History is full of these sorts of bad luck scenarios.

The reality is that despite the message of individual responsibility and accountability that has been a hallmark of the neoconservative economic mindset that has dominated our system since 1980, we are often victims of things far beyond our control. People like Chairman and CEO of Lehman Brothers Dick Fuld, Chairman of the New York Federal Reserve (and later Treasury Secretary) Timothy Geithner, and Treasury Secretary (under Bush) Hank Paulson made decisions that profoundly affected the lives of everyone on the planet and managed to completely screw over an entire generation of people in their own country. No matter where you look, there's a silent army of people responsible for the 2008 financial crisis. From Louis Rainieri, who invented mortgage-backed securities, to every person who traded in them, thousands of decisions impacted the lives of millions of people. How individualistic can we be?

It has been easy to dismiss the complaints of my generation. No one likes us, and no one ever will. We are a punchline to every joke. The word "millennial" has taken on a toxicity usually reserved for political and sex scandals. It is hard to get traction to have these conversations and realize how people have been screwed over. To some degree, this is a rejection of the cry of the collective. Instead of acknowledging the collective problem, people would sooner reject the idea of a problem than deal with the haunting realization that no matter how much individualism we might cling to, we are a collective society, and what people do in our community matters and must be a concern for us all. This is likely why socialism is quite popular with the under-45 group in the United States.

Acting collectively, especially for collaboratively minded millennials, is appealing when you realize we cannot change society to fit our view. Part of this concerns money in politics, corporate statism, or our political system. Still, much of it also has to do with the fact that we are subject to the desire for constant growth by hedge funds and investors on Wall Street and elsewhere who make decisions to enrich themselves at the collective expense. As Scott Galloway says, "Privatize the gains and socialize the losses."

Even how the 2008 crisis was handled demonstrates this problem. Banks were bailed out, but people were not. Instead of forcing all the companies to offer fixed-rate mortgages to people with variable-rate mortgages, the banks were given billions to save them. The Obama administration had an opportunity to take the banks to task, and he chose to follow the lead of Timothy Geithner and decided not to bring "Old Testament justice" to America's bankers. In the years that followed with quantitative easing (QE), assets like houses, stocks, and bonds were propped up with cheap and easy money. Calls to increase the wages of working people were met with deaf ears until the pandemic.

Years of low interest rates pumped up the stock market but rarely helped regular working people. During the pandemic, retail investing exploded as people figured out that if one could get rich playing the stock market, they might as well try it, too. It is no surprise that products like cryptocurrency have become so popular. Its entire appeal is that a decentralized currency was not controlled by the banking system that had screwed over so many people in 2008. This ability to make money from computers, technology, and math was seemingly magical for some. A new language developed around crypto trading. People could buy and sell these assets or simply hold them and ride the wave to ever higher prices and be able to afford the American dream on their own terms. "Hodling" until you "Lambo" was internet parlance used to signal that someone was going all in on a cryptocurrency—holding no matter what—until it made them enough money to buy a Lamborghini.

Millennials' problem at this stage of life is finding a way to achieve the American Dream. It seems like there is no natural way to win anymore. There is no map, and there is no clear path like there once was for us. When you look at things from this perspective, much of people's seemingly irrational behavior makes sense, even avocado toast, iPhones, and Starbucks. The problem is that despite it all, no one will ever care about these issues. Bernie Sanders popularized the idea of wealth and income inequality, but only post pandemic has the problem been taken seriously at a high level within our society. There is much conversation about the issue, but not much is being done.

There is much desperation these days. I think that is why many people are so pessimistic about the future. Talking about the world like it's on fire and society is failing all around us has become relatively common online. It has become fashionable for right-wing people in digital spaces to refute the idea and simply blame ordinary people for complaining.

The student loan discussion is also symbolic of the lack of caring around issues affecting millennials. During the pandemic, businesses were given billions of Paycheck Protection Program (PPP) loans. *The New York Times* reported in 2022 in an article titled, "Little of the Paycheck Protection Program's $800 Billion Protected Paychecks" that the program had been riddled with fraud and grift, "Jobs and businesses are two separate things," said David Autor, an economics professor at the Massachusetts Institute of Technology who led a 10-member team that studied the program. "We tried to figure out, 'Where did the money go?'—and it turns out it didn't primarily go to workers who would have lost jobs. It went to business owners and their shareholders and their creditors."

However, when it comes to providing relief for high-interest student loans, there is little desire to help. In June 2023, the Supreme Court said $10,000 of student loan debt forgiveness per individual was unconstitutional. There is no word from the high court on the constitutionality of stolen funds from the PPP.

CHAPTER 6:

MARGINALIZED MILLENNIALS

We begin with a submission from Reddit:

Here you are. Take this as a single data point, but you can take it for face value. Every word is my own. Use it as you will in your writing, or not at all (whatever helps with your book). Although I hope you can!

On my youth:

Looking back on the 2010s, decade of my youth gone by now, I can officially say I spent my entire 20s jumping from one financial crisis to the next. Constant sinking ships everywhere I went. I've known a few fulfilling relationships and even found peace with who I am, but I have never tasted financial security for more than a couple of months. It's affected my mental health in ways that I'm just now becoming aware of.

I grew up with nothing, with parents who refused to plan for a reasonable future. So I educated myself and paid for every red cent. I never grew bitter at my folks or asked for money ONCE; just always balanced doing what I was coached to do with following my personal goals.

'Don't ever take govt assistance, don't take vacations until you manage to find salaried work and save up for a home down payment. Save for retirement now. Take out as many college loans as you need. 50/30/20% rule for living/ discretionary/savings.'

Bookmarked all the personal finance blogs. Downloaded the savings apps. Read "Forbes 30 Under 30" to keep my dreams alive. Done, done and donesky. With great resilience and confidence to try, try again. Studied hundreds of articles with titles like "Everything you should start (and stop) doing as a 20-something to save for retirement." I started that Roth IRA and 401k. I graduated college with a sustainable (enough) degree. Suddenly, now when I meet people my parents' age, they smile real big and tell me "See the world while you're young. Enjoy it before you have great responsibility to stress over." Thanks. Too fucking late but thanks. I know I'll never have another youth, but all I'm searching for now are answers. No Reddit hugbox, no excuses from me or anyone else. Just, what the hell am I missing? Seriously. Whatever it is my few successful counterparts have been doing, or have internally, I am simply lacking enough of that. Thing is, I recognize a few things I could have sacrificed, daily consumption habits that weren't very conducive to savings, or maybe having the gumption to take risks and place myself in the right company at the right time....but when? Where? And with whom? I swear to God the one thing that still eludes me is how the gatekeepers of this gotcha economy expect you to be able to invest in financial risk or even save more than 5% of a paycheck at a time to ever GET off the ground. To know what the value of a dollar actually is. If I'm supposedly only worth my contribution to the GDP. They're telling us a lot of lies, at a minimum. Fuck it. If I've had the audacity to stick around til 30 with nothing to show for it but a semi stable job, I'll continue to the bitter end out of spite. Anyone else experiencing similar?

Another submission from Reddit:

Daily life from the perspective of a few of us gay 30 somethings living in middle TN:

Does anybody feel a decade behind? (Originally posted in by the same user r/AskGaybrosOver30)

Yep. '80s gaybies have an odd life timeline so far. Old enough to remember when the world was super homophobic and struggled being accepted/taught basic life skills from estranged parental and mentor figures, but young enough to have experienced things like marriage equality and majority societal acceptance during our 20s.

Things were definitely tense if you add a fundamentalist upbringing like ours. I'm 30 right now, but by the time I was out of college, I was the only one out of every gay person I knew whose parents were proudly homophobic.

As an aside, my earliest memory was mom calling a family member from a freaking rotary dialer, but by the time I graduated high school, the iPhone was released. Times change quickly.

I still cannot properly shop for groceries. It should be the simplest thing ever, but it's as if I'm learning to ride a bike at 30 and feeling lost. I have a best friend who graduated a year before me, and she's exactly the same. Married even. This is after having a good job for the better part of a year now, moving cities and securing a stable LTR (long-term relationship). I buy less than a week's worth of grub at a time. Buying anything more makes me feel almost physically nauseous, while the back of my head is preoccupied with things like car maintenance and sudden medical bills, even though I have insurance now. Call those 1st world problems but I call not being able to invest in biweekly food expenditures a serious hurdle for independent adulthood. If one can't get over that, how are they ever gonna put down for a home? Getting there one step at a time.

My older sister once found a dusty box of tax papers in my parents basement, from well before they filed online. The year my brother and I were born they net over $100k. In fucking 1989. My dad was just a blue collar union carpenter. What the HELL did they do with all of it? We never found out. I started college penniless and ended it dozens of thousands less wealthy. I'm almost his age from that time, and will almost crack 35k at the rate I'm going in sales. God help us.

Millennials are the largest generation in history. The baby boomers had many children so, as millennials hit 18 and college, American society braced for their impact on society and the workforce. Companies studied spending habits and tried to keep up with the changing tastes of millennials. Companies, industry, and anyone not a millennial has been mystified by their choices and habits. However, there is a deep economic story here to be told.

There are many stories about millennials. For the past decade, the media has become obsessed with America's largest generation. So far, millennials have killed casual dining like Applebees, Chilis, and TGI Fridays. Napkins, diamonds, and the suburbs have also become victims of millennials' refusal to participate in the greater economy. However, despite the popular news stories and the resulting social media perception, the situation is more nuanced. The numbers show that millennials aren't deliberately killing anything. There was no meeting on Instagram or Snapchat to determine what parts of the American economy would be destroyed. The simple fact is that millennials do not have the money to spend at these establishments or on these products.

The average millennial does not own their own home (although the rarity of homeownership has increased post pandemic) and does not own a new car. Despite the oldest of them being well over forty, they have less sex, use less drugs, are more faithful to their partners, and are more likely to live with their partner before marriage. The average millennial is a victim of circumstances that began long before they were born. Many of the problems millennials face began when Gen X was born in the late 1960s and 70s.

As discussed in my first book, *What the Hell is Going On?*, wages for labor remained stagnant between 1977 and 2021, although they have recently begun to rise in real terms (adjusted for inflation). There are multiple factors to why wage growth stagnated for so many years. One of the most important is that in a world where capital is valued more than labor, returns from capital will generate more wealth than labor (which was the basis of the work of Thomas Piketty). I add that this is because capital seeks a frictionless return.

For Gen X and boomers, this wage problem has presented economic difficulties because they did not create as much wealth as they might have otherwise; however, for the youngest workers, millennials, and now Gen Z, this lack of wage growth has been catastrophic. This has led many millennials to stay with their parents in their early 20s and move out with roommates well into their 30s, and, of course, this transition was deeply class-based.

When buying a home, millennials are far more likely to rely on help from family than previous generations. One of the most essential reasons that millennials coming out of the great recession are marginalized across race and, to a lesser degree, class is simple: they've been left on the economic sidelines. The effect has been to delay the normal stages of life for millennials entirely. And even worse is that Gen Z is no better off in this regard. Every trend that millennials started has only increased for Gen Z, especially after the pandemic.

One of the most tragic parts of America's lost generation is the delays in major life milestones. Among the stories sent to me, there were mentions of delaying having children or simply giving up on the idea of being able to be a parent. There was also a story from a man in his early 30s who had given up dating because he simply couldn't afford to date or give gifts. As we delve into dating later in this book, we'll see that not being able to participate in society as a regular adult or a regular person is deeply traumatizing and damaging.

All of this has led to the extreme marginalization of millennials. Every society marginalizes someone; not everyone is included. In Japanese culture, this often results in the *hikikomori* phenomenon. We'll learn more about that in the next section as we explore how Japan gave us a preview of what would happen to millennials.

In America, the results of marginalization can be even more damaging because there is little or no safety net for the marginalized amongst us. American parents aren't usually willing to humor their children's lack of success. Society isn't that kind, either. In the early days after the financial crisis, these students were ridiculed as the 1986-90 cohort of millennials moved to the safety of home amid the slowdown of the American economy. Millennials still are ridiculed for killing napkins, casual dining, cars, and home ownership.

Rather than realize that society was in crisis, Gen X and boomer politicians told millennials to figure it out. Even within families, parents sternly told their children to figure out how to put all their talents and expensive educations to work. Many people I spoke to talked about being rejected by family when they most needed them. This has caused great depression among the refugees of the 2008 financial crisis.

The impetus of this book was the economic devastation of another real estate boom: Japan in 1991. In the next section, we will take a little trip to Japan and see how an entire generation of Japanese was lost due to economic devastation and how a lack of government action and failed policies have led to terrible economic consequences at Japan's individual and societal level.

SECTION 2:

JAPAN

Japan's story of economic development is quite tremendous. In 1853, the secretive island nation opened its ports to the West. It began a process of westernization that rocketed an essentially feudalistic country into the 20th century in a matter of years. The transformation was so quick that Japan competed with the United States in the Pacific and Asia, a conflict leading to the U.S.'s entry into World War II. Japan was defeated and destroyed, but the country started an economic trajectory that seemed only to go up. Once the occupation was lifted, Japan developed an economy that seemed unstoppable—until a collapse in housing prices ended a nearly fifty-year run of remarkable growth. This had consequences for the global economy, but it also had implications for regular Japanese workers and left Japanese society changed forever in eerily familiar ways.

CHAPTER 7:

JAPAN'S LOST DECADE(S)

Japan rebuilt in the years after World War II. Hiroshima and Nagasaki were destroyed and radioactive, and Tokyo had been fire-bombed to near oblivion. However, the American occupation gave Japan a quick course in democracy and modern American capitalism. The Japanese took these lessons to heart and mastered them. Their rebuilding of the country and eventually joining the G-7, a group of elite wealthy nations, is a rags-to-riches story of a country moving from developing status to a developed, rich economy.

By the 1980s, Japan was working on buying up its former occupier. Japanese companies purchased everything they could from the Pebble Beach Golf Club to the Rockefeller Center. By the late 1980s, the Japanese ownership of major American institutions and their dominance of the automotive industry were national concerns that reached the halls of Congress and pop culture. It seemed like the Japanese could not be stopped.

A few large companies dominated the Japanese economy. These *zaibatsu* were so large that the best way to think about them is if you took the Fortune 500 companies and reduced them to the Fortune 50. Mitsubishi makes everything from car frames for Subaru to electronics and also provides banking and financial services. It's as if we merged

Goldman Sachs, General Electric, General Motors, Lockheed Martin, and Microsoft into one giant conglomerate (General-Lockheed-Sachs-Microsoft Inc). These *zaibatsu* stretch back to the waning days of feudal Japan when powerful families, free from the Tokugawa Shogunate, organized their resources into large companies to help Japan modernize in the late nineteenth century and become a modern power following the opening of Japan in 1853.

The *zaibatsu* system did not survive the war (although most of the companies did), and many new companies sprang up in the aftermath. These companies formed a *keiretsu* system in which vital parts of a given company would support the weaker parts. Competitors would own shares of each other's companies in order to avoid corporate takeovers. It was also a handy way to spread capital among companies. Imagine if General Motors held significant shares in Ford and vice versa; under the American system, that would be illegal, but that is how business is practiced in the Japanese system. This has much to do with how Japanese culture works, which we will discuss in due course.

The unstoppable Japanese economy seemed like exponential growth, and it was a given, that the wealth would continue pouring in. People in the West feared Japanese dominance in everything. Several dozen books were written throughout the 1980s proclaiming the success of the Japanese juggernaut. By 1991, it seemed like Japan wasn't just going to take over the highways of America; they were going to take over everything else, too. The Japanese economy was primarily an export economy dominated by their incredibly reliable cars and the burgeoning electronics industry. Microwaves, televisions, VHS players, cameras, and other new gadgets were all coming out of Japan. Unlike the rise of China, where American companies were the brands in charge, Japanese companies led the way with their brands like Panasonic, Toshiba, and Sony.

Michael Oswald's film *The Princes of Yen* offers a background that shows where the Japanese economy went wrong and how it left Japan with lost decades and a lost generation of people. This summarizes the film and what led to the collapse of Japanese real estate.

In the post-World War II era, the Japanese economy was stabilized by the strict control of banking, investment, and credit by the Bank of Japan. The central bank would determine where the money went in the economy, preferring specific sectors and companies. This was called Window Guidance. If the Bank of Japan wanted to invest in transport for one year, banks were encouraged to give loans in that industry at a certain quota. If then, the following year, the Bank of Japan wanted to boost construction, banks would be instructed where to loan money within their quarterly quota of loans.

In this way, the Bank of Japan somewhat planned Japan's economy. In the mid-1980s, the Bank of Japan and its titular governor, Satoshi Sumita, began work on market liberalization plans. Tadashi Sasaki, the former Bank of Japan governor, had written a five-year plan to liberalize the Japanese economy. Soon, a ten-year plan was developed. However, the Bank of Japan faced a problem: how to make market liberalization happen? For that to happen, they needed a crisis. Quantitative easing could create a bubble that, when burst, would generate the kind of crisis required.

The Ministry of Finance had little control over interest rates and the creation of new money. Any time the government inquired about the Bank of Japan's lending and other financial practices, the bankers would overwhelm them with industry jargon and complicated language that made the entire money system seem impossible to manage without the experts. Because of this opaque oversight, the Bank of Japan used its powers of Window Guidance to increase the number of loans banks would be lending by increasing their quotas and demanding they lend more money. The Japanese economy boomed. Money was flowing everywhere. Banks actively sought out people to lend money to and offered more than they were asking to borrow. The Japanese economy seemed to be going in only one direction—upward.

When Yashushi Mieno took over the Bank of Japan in 1989, he began his tenure by tightening lending. It immediately cooled the economy. In 1991, the unthinkable happened: real estate prices fell. Valuations began to fall for the first time, and soon, some assets were worth less than the loans against them. Bad debt began accumulating in banks holding the bag on this debt-fueled bubble.

The country that once boasted about land prices under the imperial palace suddenly faced a terrible economic downturn powered by heady real estate prices, especially in Tokyo. Conventional wisdom said that this was impossible. But real estate prices didn't care about conventional wisdom. Thus began an economic tailspin, making Japan an economic curiosity for the next thirty years. The Japanese juggernaut had blown a tire, and the radiator wasn't looking too good either. Subsequently, the Bank of Japan abolished Window Guidance. This meant that banks no longer knew how many loans they should issue or to whom. They had never had to make that determination before. Consequently, lending seized up, and the economy also began to fail.

In *Shutting Out the Sun*, we learn how the new slowdown and the resulting recession affected regular Japanese people. Much like how millennials were left behind due to a real estate crisis, the same happened to young Japanese students in 1991. Students in Japan, from the moment they enter school, began their journey on a giant conveyor belt that led to a lifetime job at a corporation, yearly raises based on age, and an assured retirement. Increases in wages were not tied to performance but to age.

The scholastic culture was punishing. Parents worked hard to afford the best schools so their sons (and later daughters) could go to the best universities, get good grades, and get excellent, safe corporate jobs. The legendary Japanese salaryman (and until the late 1970s it was men) was the goal for Japanese students in university. However, a similar system was even applied for Japanese workers not in university. After finishing a vocational program, a worker would rely on the fact that once he was on the assembly line at Toyota City, he would be on the assembly line, or within the company, until retirement with small raises and a possibility for advancement into supervisory roles. This is a big part of Japanese identity; many Japanese will introduce themselves with their company name first.

In 1993, companies began to do the unthinkable: they laid people off. For a Japanese worker, getting a new job is not as easy as simply crossing the street to the company hiring and getting a new job. Any lapse in employment is a veritable death sentence in the Japanese working world. For recent graduates, not being recruited right out of school was an early exit from the conveyor belt and made getting a good job nearly impossible. Much of Japanese working culture is based on social connections. Getting a new job means trying to break into already established social networks that have been years in the making.

In 1991, the lifetime employment system that had dominated Japanese working life collapsed. Japanese companies never returned to the former system either. It was reported in the *Nikkei Asian Review* in an article from 2018 titled, "Lost generation Haunts Japan, Abe, and the BOJ," that Japanese companies drastically reduced their recruitment of graduates from 1993 to 2004. For Japanese students today, doing well in school is essential for the simple hope that a big company might recruit them. This has made Japanese schools even more cutthroat than they already were.

The comparisons between what happened in Japan in 1991 and what happened in America in 2008 are stark. We have all the pieces: a falling real estate market after a long bubble of economic growth, students being left behind and out of the employment market, and little help for them to get on the employment or property ladder and start families of their own.

The *Nikkei Asian Review* also wrote a bleak article in 2019 called "Nightmare 2040: Japan's Lost Generation" which reported that of the 23 million people born between 1970 and 1982 who came of age during Japan's employment ice age, "550,000 are unemployed and another 700,000 are involuntary regular workers," in numbers from Yusuki Shimoda, the chief economist at the Japan Research Institute. The article goes on to tell the story of Takeshi Erikawa, the "great bureaucrat," admits that this is a significant problem and that the only solution is to employ these people in areas that are desperate for labor, like tourism, agriculture, and forestry. He proposes that a local consumption tax could fund the whole transition. He admits that retraining people in their 30s and 40s is not easy but these quasi-government jobs could be just the answer. At least he knows how to help Japan's lost generation. No one in the U.S. has suggested anything so bold for millennials left behind from the Great Recession.

According to *Japan Today*, in a 2019 article titled "Japan's lost generation facing bleak future," 900,000 Japanese workers were left behind. That's not a massive number in a nation of 127 million, but it's large enough to cause concern for the Japanese government. These workers have no savings or investments and struggle to make ends meet. When the employment market broke, they were forced into part-time employment that paid minimally and gave them no real chance for advancement. They will rely entirely on the Japanese pension system, which will likely not be enough to support them in a thirty-year retirement. Given Japan's aging crisis and falling birth rates, another question is where the workers will come from to support the pension regime.

The economic life for those affected by the 1991 crisis is challenging even for the employed Japanese worker of the same age. In the "Lost Generation Haunts Japan, Abe, and the BOJ" article, Naoko Kuga, a senior researcher at the NLI Research Institute, reported depressed spending throughout the Japanese economy. Workers aged 40 to 44 are prone to spend money on children's education, vacations, and dining, but that spending is depressed because they make 6.8 percent less than their counterparts only ten years older. They are promoted less because graduates who made it out before the employment ice age are still climbing the ladder, and there is simply no room for them or the higher salaries they could be earning.

These conditions created a lost generation of Japanese who could never recover economically from the 1991 real estate collapse and the resulting recession. However, Japanese people in their early careers would also have another situation to deal with. The next economic threat would not come from the Bank of Japan but from a nearby neighbor.

CHAPTER 8:

THE ASIAN FINANCIAL CRISIS

Japanese young people would not have much time to recover from the real estate crisis of 1991. Although the Japanese economy made marginal improvements through 1993, the economy shifted into recession again, and soon, another financial crisis would rock the world and Japan. By 1997, the Japanese economy was already having a hard time. Employment was down, the yen was deflated, and the Japanese economy faltered. It had been four long years of recession, even as the U.S. and other western countries had rapid economic expansion.

The Thai baht (Thai currency) collapsed in 1997 due to the Thai government floating their currency because they could no longer peg it to the U.S. dollar. Without the artificial peg, the value of the baht collapsed, and that triggered a financial crisis throughout the region. In Tokyo, Yamaichi Securities, founded in 1897, collapsed amid the crisis. Japan's oldest securities house had provided the financing for the 1964 Olympics and much of the post-war rebuilding. Shohei Nozawa took to the media and begged the nation's forgiveness for billions in hidden losses. William Pesek, author of the book *Japanization*, reported that as political theater, the performance could not be beaten.

The start of this crisis triggered a flight of capital and a currency crisis throughout Southeast Asia. Stock prices surged and then fell. From Tokyo to Singapore and Seoul, to Bangkok and Jakarta, markets roiled as currencies lost value and foreign investors who had poured money into the region pulled out their deposits and demanded cash. This capital crisis left the regional banks with diminishing reserves, defaulting loans, and insufficient capital to cover payments and other obligations. Credit markets soon seized up, and the biggest banks in the region simply ran out of money.

This had a terrible effect on the local economies of all the nations involved. Companies went under because they could not access credit. The International Monetary Fund (IMF) came to the rescue to provide loans to stop the crisis. However, as we know from the Greek debt crisis, the IMF always insists on market liberalization, open capital flows, and less regulation. These conditions would invite international investors to return to the troubled banks. What resulted was a fire sale of assets throughout the region in the late 1990s.

Market liberalization emerged from the currency crisis and became the preferred economic model. Shareholder capitalism reached the Japanese shore in 1997 as the Asian Financial Crisis raged. The IMF only gave loans to countries that agreed with structural reform. All the Southeast Asian markets, with the notable exception of Malaysia, embraced these reforms. Prime Minister Koizumi announced that there would be no growth until reform. Tax incentives were given to stock purchases, and the worst aspects of American capitalism took over the Japanese economy. Hedge funds bought up risky assets and failed businesses, stripping them of assets and selling them off or simply closing them.

There is an important connection between the Asian financial crisis and the 2008 crash. One person participated in both rescues: Timothy Geithner. As undersecretary of the Treasury, he had worked under David Rubin; by 2008, he had become governor of the Federal Reserve Bank of New York and was first on the scene when the big investment banks started failing. The fire sale of Bear Sterns, according to PBS Frontline, was straight out of the Asian financial crisis playbook.

Japan would close out the 1990s in weak economic conditions. The Asian Financial Crisis created a double-dip recession that lasted until the turn of the new millennium. Deflation soon became Japan's biggest problem. Interest rates were lowered to zero percent to try to stimulate inflation. Still, the Bank of Japan, until the pandemic, could not generate the needed inflation to cause the economy to grow. This was partly due to increased government debt and the high savings rate of the Japanese people.

CHAPTER 9:

JAPANIZATION

When I started writing this book in 2020, the prospect of the Japanization of the American economy seemed like a far-off problem, possible for the 2030s. However, thanks to inflation and a tight labor market, the American economy is hurtling toward a Japanese-like situation at lightning speed. The word stagflation has been thrown around when comparing the present U.S. economic situation to the late 1970s when we faced high inflation, stagnating wages, and little economic growth. Japan is a cautionary tale. Japan has never economically recovered from the crash of 1991, and one lost decade turned into three.

One of the chief problems with Japan is the years of deflation. With the pandemic and a steep rise in inflation worldwide, Japan lucked out. Japan needed inflation. The danger is, at least according to William Pesek in his book *Japanization*, that Japan's borrowing costs on its debt service will run out of control and bankrupt the government, which will either have to raise taxes or print money, causing hyperinflation like in Zimbabwe. Pesek quotes Barry Bosworth from the Brookings Institute, "Will the United States do better? Since the financial crisis, the U.S.'s economic situation has taken on many of the characteristics of Japan."

To echo Peter Zeihan, Japan is the worst country regarding demographics. Japan is a rapidly aging society with a shrinking population and an abysmal birth rate. Immigration is complex because Japan is a relatively homogenous society. Although Japan does import workers from Southeast Asia on a seasonal basis, Japan does not offer them residency. The government has tried to change these politics, but whether Japanese companies will be willing to hire these new workers who have residence, and later their children, remains to be seen. This is an area where the U.S. has an advantage, but how long that might last remains to be seen. Immigration under the Trump administration nearly dried up, only to come roaring back under Biden to exceed levels from the Obama administration. If America's jingoistic tendencies continue, a valuable source of revitalization and future workers could be cut off.

The risk of Japanization looms large. Pesek compares Japan and the United States when he writes, "Japan's is a tale of hubris and missed opportunities. Rather than quickly scrapping a model based on over-investment, exports, and excessive debt, Tokyo delayed change at all costs by relying on current-account surpluses, huge budget deficits, and asset bubbles. In many ways, it still does. Does this sound familiar?" Yes, it does, Mr. Pesek. It sounds like every policy the Federal Reserve and the government have pursued since 2008 across four presidential administrations. Pesek continues the comparison, "Many economists would argue that the period following 2008, after the crash of Lehman Brothers and many of Wall Street's biggest players, ushered in the start of at least a semi-lost decade for the United States."

There is also the idea that the problem did not begin in the run-up to the financial crisis, but that 2008 was merely an exposure of the rot within the system. Within Pesek's book, there is another argument from Larry Summers, "The crux of Summer's argument was this: The global crisis that nearly bankrupted Wall Street in 2008 was a highly odd one, and not just because of its size and brutality. At the time, many experts and economic pundits believed monetary policy, at least dating back to the days of the Greenspan Fed, had been too lax. The banking system was filled with imprudent lending policies and securities, and households began to feel richer than they were. The conventional wisdom was that there was too much liquidity, too much credit being extended, and too much paper wealth being created." And there is something to be said for this argument.

During his long tenure as chairman of the Federal Reserve, Alan Greenspan continued the work of his mentor, Paul Volcker, by keeping inflation and unemployment low at two percent, essentially the twin pillars of the Federal Reserve mandate from Congress. However, as Greenspan admitted in the aftermath of the 2008 crisis, he had found "a flaw" in the system he had so carefully orchestrated for 20 years. Summers identified the problem. The economic growth after the stagflation of the 1970s did not come from productive investment but from financialization. Consumers spent more money, not because they were being paid more but because banks extended ever larger lines of credit. Having credit debt was practically a fashion in the 1990s. Credit consolidation became a whole new industry. Credit scores were introduced in 1989 to help banks decide who could get better rates and credit. People felt wealthier, but they weren't wealthier. It was all built on credit and not rising wages.

The social implications of this are quite dire. Looking at the situation in Japan with the *hikikomori*, a pension fund crisis, and rising homelessness, it is easy to see those years of lagging economic growth, lack of job opportunities, and an unequal society can lead to consequences for everyone. The unemployed young people of Japan in 1991 and the U.S. in 2008 become middle-aged adults and senior citizens with lower lifetime earnings and less saved (if any) for retirement. These people become dependent on ever more state aid to survive, stressing governments with a financial burden they are ill-equipped to meet.

Financial crisis and social stagnation can also be deadly. According to Pesek, "But the downfall of Japan's oldest securities house in 1997 offers a variety of fascinating bookends. Between 1997 and 1998, for example, a year of historic upheaval and big layoffs, Japan's suicide rate jumped 35 percent and has remained around 30,000 per year ever since."

When I started writing this book, the prospect of the U.S. becoming more like Japan seemed a far-off possibility. In the intervening three years, it has become a stark reality. What if the lost decade in Japan becomes the global norm? Ronnie Chan, chairman of Hang Lang Properties Ltd, said at the Asia Innovation Initiate conference held on July 8, 2008, "Can you imagine that? Perhaps we should. Perhaps people should get used to slower growth or no growth."

Given how much of the economy is predicated on growth over time, slow growth or no growth scenario seems the most frightening. An exit must be found to avoid the scenario that Jeremy Grantham, cofounder of the global investment management fund GMO LLC, fears—that pretty much every asset class, everywhere in the world, is in the midst of a bubble of some kind and that each imbalance reinforces another. "Sustained strong fundamentals and sustained easy credit go on better: They allow for continued reinforcement," the Boston-based Grantham argued. "The more leverage you take, the better you do. The better you do, the more leverage you take."

Combining these situations with an age of cheap money, which lasted from 2008 to 2022, leaves the U.S. economy in a perilous state. Ben Bernanke's quantitative easing experiment was another question mark. Over time, the Federal Reserve will find that politicians, bankers, investors, and business people get addicted to free money too quickly and clamor for more. Once central banks start embracing assets such as corporate debt, commercial paper, mortgage-backed securities, exchange-traded funds, real estate trusts, and the like, they tend to get stuck. This has undoubtedly come to be the case. As inflation increased due to pandemic spending, the Federal Reserve rapidly raised interest rates in 2022 and 2023 to control inflation and slow the economy. The price of everything shot up. Japan had a different problem in the 1990s; rather than being fueled by cheap money after the crisis, Japan couldn't generate inflation, no matter how low interest rates got. The Bank of Japan was the first central bank to offer zero percent interest rates, but that did nothing to ease the deflation of the Japanese economy.

CHAPTER 10:

LESSONS FROM THE LAND OF THE RISING SUN

Thanks to a random YouTube video I found, I started to think about the Japanese situation with their lost generation. This launched me onto a research binge that resulted in this book. I wanted to use the experience of Japan's lost generation to show what happens when a generation simply fails to launch and the societal, economic, and social consequences of that economic fallout. Often, a problem can be clarified by looking at it through a different lens. To understand the American crisis and how we created a lost generation, we must take a short flight to Tokyo.

One of the outstanding situations that is troubling about our Japanese cousins is how little the government of Japan has done to improve their situation. Like the United States, the Bank of Japan has tried to fix the Japanese economy through various monetary policies. Successive governments have come and gone without ever solving the problem: people who came of age in the early 1990s just don't have the money they need to support Japan's economy. This was covered quite well by the 2018 *Nikkei Asian Review* article titled "Lost Generation Haunts Japan, Abe, and BOJ," previously mentioned in Chapter 7.

Although the Japanese lost generation precedes the American, many underlying causes are the same. In the next chapter, I'll dig into the specifics. Still, the reality is that these two wealthy, developed nations caused economic crises that affected millions of lives. Both governments have been slow to act to stave off the crisis, if they acted at all. Declines in real estate and shaky financial institutions caused the 1991 Japanese and 2008 American crashes. Both followed great economic expansions, leaving millions of young people looking for answers when there weren't any to be found.

What is most depressing is that Japan had fifteen years to figure out how to increase the number of people who came into the job market in 1991, and they haven't created a program or incentive to help people find better jobs or get back into Japanese corporate life, despite plenty of promises from various governments. This doesn't paint much of a shining picture for millennials. Like the Japanese, those Americans born a little before or after the millennial birth years are faring better. There are still downstream effects, though. Workers who entered the Japanese workforce later have endured a lackluster economy with nearly no growth, and expensive living costs, especially in Tokyo. The years have ticked by, and people have struggled through "the employment ice age."

In Pesek's *Japanization*, he writes, "Japan's is a tale of hubris and missed opportunities. Rather than quickly scrapping a model based on over-investment, exports, and excessive debt, Tokyo delayed change at all costs by relying on current account surpluses, huge budget deficits, and asset bubbles. In many ways, it still does. Does this sound familiar?"

In Michael Zielenziger's *Shutting Out the Sun*, we begin to get a picture of the situation. Zielenziger wrote:

> As a result of satellite TV, foreign film, and overseas vacations, young Japanese are waking up to the imbalances and inadequacies so apparent to outsiders in their rich nation. They now see how others live, how young people in other

nations tend to take greater control over their lives but having never been taught or given the incentive to think critically, and lacking any social mechanism that would allow them to revel, all too many of the young—those in their twenties, thirties, and forties, who should be helping Japan readjust and realign its society to the realities of the information age—are, like the *hikikomori*, finding ultimately self-destructive ways to detach from that society. The suicide rate has risen precipitously, while women in growing numbers are saying no to marriage and motherhood. Youth unemployment is stuck at an all-time high. Alcoholism, depression, and divorce are increasing. Violence among teenagers grows more pronounced, and grade school children, some as young as eleven, kill classmates in sudden snaps of rage, known as *kireru*. Colonies of blue plastic tarps, the spontaneous tent cities erected by thousands of homeless, have sprouted like dandelions in Tokyo's biggest parks and are visible along railway embankments and underpasses. Family life is fraying. Faced with such bleak prospects, many young adults hide out in cults that obsess over pursuing brand-name goods or retreat into pop culture and cartoons.

Does that sound familiar with what millennials and Gen Z face here in the United States?

CHAPTER 11:

CONSEQUENCES

We must first travel east to Japan to understand the long-term consequences of a lost generation. Japan is a formal society in a style unique to Asian cultures. Their value of community and society over the individual is unfamiliar in the West, where the individual takes primacy. It is this fundamental cultural difference that makes many of the consequences of the Japanese economic collapse begin to come into focus.

In *Shutting Out the Sun*, Zielenziger says of the Japanese plight:

> On a deeper level, however, the decline of a great power like Japan is relevant—or cautionary—to citizens of other great nations, who, like Americans, wonder whether their society, too, might someday lose its vital gift for reinvention and renewal. Like the United States, Japan has for decades been pampered in material comforts, coddled by its hubris, and sheltered in its own technological sophistication. Like America, it believes that only its unique ways of conducting business and interacting with the world—methods that were so effective throughout its history—can continue to sustain a sense of blessed superiority.... Also, like Americans,

Japanese face the paradoxical challenge that wealth creates. For only in societies blessed with unrivaled prosperity do people have the luxury to consider what it is that truly makes them happy.

Workers who graduated are still struggling today and competing with colleagues who are just a few years older. In the article, "Lost Generation Haunts Japan, Abe and the BOJ" from the *Nikkei Asian Review* there is a powerful quote, "In our company, there just aren't any positions for us to get promoted to,' said a 40-year-old man working for a major financial institution in Tokyo. He and colleagues around his age frequently complain about their dim prospects for earning promotions and raises, he said." The article goes on to say that "People in their 40s are more likely to spend on houses or children's education, but that is being suppressed," explained Naoko Kuga, senior researcher at the NLI Research Institute. "Avoidable spending, such as family vacations and dining out, is also suppressed. Normally, when workers see no avenue to promotion, they have the option of seeking a new job with a better salary. But this, too, is a tall order in Japan, due to the country's unique hiring practices and wage systems. Companies typically prefer to hire new graduates, leaving few openings for older workers. Yet age discrimination is rarely, if ever discussed."

Does any of this sound familiar to the plight of millennials? The oldest millennials are in their early 40s now, and while the American economy is more dynamic and larger than Japan's, Japanese workers who graduated into that recession are still struggling. The *Japan Times* reported in 2018, in an article titled, "Japan's Ice Age Generation Urges Revamp of State Hiring Push," "According to government data, there were 16.89 million people in Japan between 35 and 44—the cohort comprising the generation—in 2018. Of them, 3.71 million were employed on a nonregular basis, with 500,000 seeking regular jobs, and about 400,000 were not engaged in employment, household labor or studies. About 9.16 million held regular jobs."

SHUTTING AWAY

The Japanese phenomenon of *hikikomori* seems unique to Japan. This group of men, and it is primarily men, have entirely abandoned Japanese society and locked themselves away in the rooms of their parents' homes. South Korea has a similar phenomenon, but their requirement of two years of national service breaks these young men out of their homes and forces them into military life. In Japan, where military service isn't required, these young men are pretty lost.

Their plight belies a greater problem within Japanese society. Zielenziger wrote:

> Yet many gifted young Japanese like Jun yearn for distinctive careers and grasp for means to articulate their aspirations. Japanese magazines sometimes describe it in glowing terms as 'I-turn' rather than U-turn refugees, that is, disaffected urban workers who return to the countryside of their grandparents to grow organic foods and reclaim traditional Japanese *yakimono* or ceramics. Surveys among schoolchildren show they are no longer fixated on becoming businessmen or bureaucrats: more kids today say they want to grow up to be cooks, carpenters, or solitary craftsmen.' For any *hikikomori* he (Jun) told me, the challenge is to preserve your inner feelings and unique identity while still finding a way to function in the larger world of the collective. 'When *hikikomori* try to adapt themselves to the demands of the economic society, they have to destroy their insides,' he told me months later when he was deeply engaged in his own book. 'To survive in Japan, you have to kill off your own original voice.'

In *Shutting Out the Sun*, we do see how the punishing culture of Japanese schools and corporations can shut out anyone who doesn't fit in. Some young men flee Japan to Canada, the United States, or even nearby countries like Thailand in order to escape the Japanese system and live their own lives.

Back here in the United States, we have our own situation with youthful antipathy, although not quite as severe as what Japan faces with its young men who hide from the world. NEETs (Not in Employment, Education or Training) avoid work because it seems pointless and offers no opportunity for any sort of life. The phrase NEET is not a new term. One can easily find these people online, and the situation seems rather dire.

However, after reviewing some of the things people in the NEET community have posted about themselves on Reddit, the mood in the community is dire. Many don't feel like they fit into society or that society has a place for them because society seems to have left them behind. With no hope for a future and no clear pathway into being a part of society or dating, despair soon sets in.

This isn't entirely an economic story. Many people consciously reject regular life and choose to stay home and shun society. Claims of autism or other mental health issues are also present in the community. These disorders make socialization difficult and interacting with other humans in a way that will be recognized as acceptable and not found strange. (Negative experiences abound in the community.) There is also a smattering of agoraphobia.

There is an economic story as well, but it's not in the area that one might think. Complaints of being unattractive and lacking physical features playing into job hiring decisions are expected. Difficulty interviewing because of social anxieties is present as well. These complaints extend to the claim that good social connections are needed to get employment beyond the minimum wage, which is also common. These complaints have some basis. Having an extensive professional network is found in nearly every job-seeking advice article for a reason. The person recommended by an existing employee often fares better in getting an interview or being hired. Attractiveness in hiring has some scientific basis. A University of Buffalo study in

2021 titled "Is beauty more than skin deep? Attractiveness, power, and nonverbal presence in evaluations of hirability" by Min-Hsuan Tu, Elisabeth K. Gilbert, Joyce E. Bono report that, "Although prior research has suggested that bias on the part of evaluators is the source of attractive individuals' favorable career outcomes, there is also evidence that these individuals may be socialized to behave and perceive themselves differently from others in ways that contribute to their success. Building on socialization research and studies on nonverbal power cues, we examined nonverbal communication in individuals with varying degrees of physical attractiveness. In two experimental studies with data from 300 video interview pitches, we found that attractive individuals had a greater sense of power than their less attractive counterparts and thus exhibited a more effective nonverbal presence, which led to higher managerial ratings of their hirability." A similar study from Harvard in 2005 entitled "Why Beauty Matters" echoes the same sentiment, although without emphasizing power position and socialization.

However, looking at this community, another aspect of the economic story develops. What if these people lived in a country with a better education system and a functioning economy that produced good-paying jobs with dignity and respect? What if these people had free access to healthcare and mental health services? What if a government service was dedicated to helping those who have fallen off the conveyor belt of life to get back on it in their own way? What if there were higher education options that didn't plow young people into thousands of dollars of debt? Would it save everyone? No. Would it save many? Quite possibly.

OLD AGE

Because of the economic devastation of the Lost Decade, Japan now faces a pension crisis by 2040 as the people from that generation begin to retire and call upon a system that they have not paid into and which is slowly becoming insolvent. Many workers were shunted into low-paying jobs and either didn't pay into the pension system or didn't pay in enough, leaving nearly a million people with no retirement possibilities and leaving the pension system nearing a breaking point because of the lack of money flowing into the system.

Here in the United States, we face a crisis with Social Security. With the fund set to run out of money sometime from 2035 to 2040 (depending on estimates), it will be barely able to help Gen X (whose retirement age will be 67, not 65), and it may not exist in any form for millennials. This has led people to quip on Twitter/X that suicide is their retirement plan. The Japanese are already implementing that policy with a suicide rate of 30,000 per year. What do you do when it seems like life is impossible?

SECTION 3:

WORK

Employment is an area where millennials have struggled for most of their adulthood. To many, it seemed that getting a good-paying job was practically impossible without family or other connections. This has been a common experience for various people, like the person in this submission from Reddit:

> When I graduated from college in 2015, I sent out applications and did interviews for months. Eventually I went broke and started delivering sandwiches to the same offices I had tried to get a job in. I lived in a state capital at the time and had a degree in economics and public administration. But ironically I couldn't even get an internship. It was a difficult period of my life, and it made me bitter for awhile. Luckily, I was able to regroup, financially and emotionally, and get on a different professional path. But I had to totally sacrifice my 20s to the god of money to get it done. I don't have a single friend left. All I care about is working because I'm so scared of being broke again.

CHAPTER 12:

MODERN WORK CULTURE

The Great Resignation has undoubtedly demonstrated that Americans have had it with an exploitative and abusive work culture, which is not just an American problem. In Asia, the "lay flat" movement is as popular as the quiet quitting movement. Since the pandemic, people have re-evaluated their relationship with work and desired a work-life balance that hasn't existed for the past forty years. In this submission from Reddit, we see how people live through these conditions.

> 28F. People should not have to go back to school multiple times in their life to leave skilled and important fields that America desperately needs. An example being my fiancé who was an EMT making $10.75 and myself who wanted to be an elementary education teacher most of my young life.
>
> I was told I had to "pull myself up from my bootstraps and get a better job", as if teaching wasn't even...needed. Like it wasn't a "real job" that deserved pay. I went from working briefly at a strip club because I was so desperate for the money. I busted so hard to go back to school and go into aerospace. I'm only making $18 an hour. I shouldn't have

had to give up teaching to make $18 an hour. Jobs are requiring more and more but giving less and less.

I guess I don't live in poverty as I have some savings, but I don't have much. At this point I will never have a house. Zero plans to have a kid even though our main goal was to adopt. I could never afford adoption either. Fiancé and I have been living together for 10 years and just now engaged with no actual real plans for the wedding because we can't afford one. The push for STEM (Science, Technology, Engineering, and Math) and how big of a moneymaker was always a facade pushed by a generation of workers whose work and pay no longer exist. Most electrician and hands-on jobs barely come close to paying $18 an hour in Florida and also usually require you own a truck and your own tools.

I'm a radio frequency tester and see many lesser jobs paying more. Even in a specialized and niche field such as aerospace, I witness women being paid less and young people treated as expendable as well as older people being totally expendable and gotten rid of despite their knowledge.

DECLINING UNIONIZATION AND STAGNANT WAGES

In my essay "1977: The Rise of Discounters and Deregulation," I talked extensively about the stagnant wage problem American workers have faced since 1977. This wage gap was covered over by the reduction in the prices of tangible goods powered by globalization and moving production overseas with cheaper labor costs. These goods were sold back to Americans and Europeans at discounter stores like Walmart, Target, and their international counterparts. People in developed countries felt richer because things were cheaper, but the reality is that they were getting poorer.

Reagan broke the back of American labor when he fired all the air traffic controllers in 1983 and banned them from federal employment for life. This was when American unions quit fighting the trend of deregulation in various industries. It was better to keep the job than to be fired wholesale. Unionization peaked in 1960 at forty-nine percent of workers. Today, that number stands at thirteen percent (although it is rising slowly). Unions signed on to worse deals that put more employee expense on the back of the worker, not on the corporation. Phrases like "making us more competitive" and "fairer to the customer" were much ballyhooed, but they had little to do with competitiveness or fairness. It represented a massive wealth transfer from the worker to the owner class. However, this change of attitude has made a select individuals few fabulously wealthy.

Changing the relationship between companies and workers allowed American businesses to adopt the Jack Welch model of fetishizing shareholder value above all other considerations. Executives' pay increased, and the stock market rose precipitously. After the difficult years of the 1970s, it seemed like the American economy was back on track. Americans felt richer. Alan Greenspan seemed to be the master of the economic universe until it all fell apart.

The reality is that this period of prosperity was not because people were getting richer. Far from it, the average worker was getting poorer by the year. The only people getting richer were those who worked in the C-suites of major corporations and their stockholders. The easy availability of credit through reduced banking regulation and the promotion of home ownership made it seem like things were improving when they weren't. In 2008, this house of cards came tumbling down and revealed what Alan Greenspan would describe in a 2008 congressional hearing before the Senate Finance Committee as "a flaw."

David Blanchflower, a British-American labor economist and academic at Dartmouth, wrote in his book *Not Working: Where Have All the Good Jobs Gone?*, "The high-paying union private sector jobs for the less educated are long gone. Real weekly wages in February 2019 in the United States were around 9 percent below their 1972 peak for private-sector production and non-supervisory workers in constant 1982-1984 dollars. In the UK, real wages in 2018 are 6 percent below their 2008 level." He then summarizes the problem: "The relatively high living standards of the least educated Americans used to be much higher than that of the less educated in Europe, for example, in the 1960s and 1970s. Perhaps no longer as with the global competition, we may see a great equalizing."

Blanchflower immediately shows that such an equalizing is happening in the UK. After an interview with the plant manager of a large EU multinational, he wrote, "When I subsequently asked him about the next pay round, he told me there wasn't going to be one. When I asked why not, he said, 'Because the workers there know the East Europeans would like their jobs and would do them better for less money.'"

This is the employment dynamic that all millennials, especially working-class millennials, face.

WHERE ARE THE ENTRY-LEVEL JOBS?

In his book *The Theft of a Decade: How the Baby Boomers Stole the Millennials' Economic Future*, Joseph C. Sternberg, an editor and political economist for the European edition of the Wall Street Journal, says of early career jobs, "How well someone starts early in their career can greatly determine their overall career trajectory. This ranges from promotions to earnings. Often, those first 2-5 years of working life will determine how things go down the path of life." Sternberg writes, "The most important benefit millennials are missing out on as they get locked out of traditional employment is an employer's investment on their training and skills. As a cohort, millennials might have more education than any previous generation. However, like any previous generation, we still need to learn how to translate that education into real, on-the-job competence in the working world. Entry-level jobs in which an employer might start to invest in providing some of the coaching and mentoring that fully bakes a young worker are disappearing to be replaced by gig jobs that exist precisely because employers don't think they can economically invest in providing on-the-job training to a promising, green full-time employee."

Unpaid internships have been a bane for students for decades, but only in recent years have they come under scrutiny. Sternberg wrote in *The Theft of a Decade*, "Unpaid interns essentially self-finance their own training in the workplace. This is a particularly pernicious trend from a social perspective because this method of entry-level training favors young adults whose families have the money to navigate the labyrinth of internship applications and the financial means to support a young adult who's working for free." He continued, "That might have prevented some of the worst abuses in the internship job market, but none of these measures fundamentally improve the incentives for companies to invest in productivity enhancements and training for workers instead of trying to replace as much labor as possible."

For working-class millennials, an unpaid internship was simply not possible. It was a struggle for the middle-class kids, leaving the upper class and wealthy kids to slot themselves into the opportunities that would advance their careers. It also allowed companies to offload their training costs onto the employees. This has been a feature of corporate America for the past forty years. They were shifting costs onto anyone else other than the corporate balance sheet.

MILLENNIAL WORKING LIFE

The lack of entry-level jobs and the early career struggle that many millennials faced in the 2009-2013 period led to millennials losing three to five years of work experience in their 20s, leaving them a significant but poorly skilled generation, according to Peter Zeihan. This has somewhat hobbled the American workforce and has certainly hobbled millennials' wages and ability to build wealth like their parents or Gen X cousins. The lack of entry-level jobs was compounded by the internship system where young people worked for free unnecessarily for companies who could afford to hire them for "experience." The job market was tight as millennials entered the workforce, and companies, through internships, were (and still are) getting free labor from young people.

Imagine this: you're young, you're talented, you've gone to school, and you're ready to hit the streets for your first job. You find a few listings and then see something that fits you perfectly; the descriptions sound like you wrote it about yourself. There's just one catch: it doesn't pay. Your heart sinks, and you move on, hoping to find something better. Nothing comes up, you are getting frantic, the bills are piling up, and something is better than nothing, right? It might lead to something, right? It has to be better than working fast food, right? So you move back in with your parents and reduce your expenses to a minimal amount. You take that internship or low-paying job and start working for free, hoping that employment will be right around the corner. But what happens when that employment never comes after two or more internships? How much longer can you keep working hard for no compensation?

Although it hasn't done much good, various lawyers and activists have been working to end the harmful practice of bringing in entry-level workers without compensation. They filed lawsuits against former employers and only charged clients when they recovered the lost wages. When I first wrote about this in 2014, I found several places tackling this legal issue; almost all have closed or move on to other matters. At the time, news outlets of a wide variety highlighted the perils of the younger generation trying to figure out how to make it in a tight job market with few opportunities.

Under the legal definition, interns should only do tasks and jobs that support their learning process about their job and field. What's more, the business is supposed to gain no direct benefit from the intern. Bringing people in to make coffee, run photo copies, and do other menial tasks (actual work) does not further their learning process in their fields. Ask anyone who has ever taken an internship; interns do much actual work, especially in competitive internships. Internships don't always equal jobs; interns often work at a company for free. Worse yet, they get paid in ways that don't pay bills like "connections" and "exposure." Working at a company for free in the hopes that it will turn into something is often a losing game despite the success of a few. It is time for this practice to stop and for companies to follow the existing labor law around internships. I know for myself I have spent much time working for free and doing real work for no compensation while bills and obligations went unpaid.

This movement has spun into a whole activist community helping people recover stolen wages (times they worked for free), and lobbying for raising the minimum wage, which is a proposal that has been voted on in several states and passed. The working world should be fair, a fair day's wage for a fair day's work; even the Republicans can get on board with that.

Labor costs have been one of the most extensive areas of cost-cutting in corporate America over the last forty years. Since 1977, wages have stagnated and no longer have risen with productivity. Sternberg says, "The percentage of economic output paid to workers as compensation during the 1950s and 60s hovered above 64 percent; that proportion, called the labor share, has been declining for most of the time since then." It is now at around 44 percent. Where has that money gone? Into the pockets of the wealthiest Americans.

Sternberg explains why the job market is so tricky. "It seems increasingly plausible that this transformation not only changed the mix between machines and labor within companies but then changed the types of jobs companies created as they needed to hire employees with the skills to make use of the most up-to-date technologies. This explains several of the labor market trends that have plagued millennials. The most highly skilled cohort of young workers are prospering.

But most younger workers are in greater risk of being crowded out of the labor market by older workers, who will have more skills and experience with which to make the best use of new technologies. Part of the explanation is that unionized workers are able to price younger, less experienced workers out of the market."

There have been some adverse economic changes as well. Sternberg says, "The Affordable Care Act ratcheted up the cost of hiring new employees especially among smaller and medium-sized firms." In addition, productivity has been flat since the Great Financial Crisis, and the pandemic, and it has decreased for the first time since World War II. "Oren Cass, an economist at the right-leaning Manhattan Institute for Policy Research, makes a convincing argument in *The Once and Future Worker* that over this span (boomers' lifetimes) the United States transformed from a production economy into a consumption economy."

Most of the jobs between 2009 and the start of the pandemic were in the service industry, where a college degree was not required in most cases. Take, for example, someone who tends a bar—at a decent bar, they would earn a very livable wage, possibly middle class. Meanwhile, a teacher whose starting salary is only $27,500 a year and requires a college degree would make considerably less than a bartender. As one friend who was making the transition said, "I'm taking a pay cut from my current job (bartending)."

But this social media trend is a reaction to a system that advantages capital over workers. Millennials in the service sector have been on the front lines of the worst practices companies have used to get the most work out of the fewest people.

Much like its logistical cousin, "just in time stocking," "just in time scheduling" tries to make sure that any business, especially retail environments, has only the people required at any given time. For workers, this can mean unpredictable hours and split shifts. Many workers in service industries, especially before the pandemic, were on a part-time basis (less than twenty-nine hours) to avoid paying mandatory medical benefits required by the Affordable Care Act.

The "clopen" is a classic retail and restaurant scheduling tactic where the person who closed the night before must arrive the following day to open up the shop or eatery again. For example, a store might close at nine p.m. and open again at eight a.m. A clopen happens when the same person is standing behind the counter again less than twelve hours later. These practices were so bad that social media began circulating posts from workers about not even bothering to go home because they would get home in time to have a few fitful hours of sleep and then return to work.

Unsurprisingly, many resented the pandemic-era regulations on service workers and how quickly they were deemed essential. Becoming an essential worker did not shield them from any of the above practices, and it rarely resulted in any pay increase. Some workers in some places were given "hero pay," but that was far from a panacea. Certainly, the stimulus checks from the government were helpful. Still, the reality is that these people were on the front lines of the pandemic, were the first to be infected, and often were many of the casualties, especially in the early days.

Lean staffing has even affected office workers. In one of my office jobs, I did the work of at least three or four people on a small staff of thirteen. My day would range from answering phones for a hotline and answering people's questions to taking online chats to writing and editing marketing and editorial copy to create new digital systems. In another day and time, that would have been a variety of jobs, but instead, it fell onto one person. This was common in this office, and it had been for years. Many articles will talk about the burnout of American workers. Still, many will not cite the true source: companies have been understaffing for years, saving millions and billions in labor costs and passing on the benefits, not to their workers but instead to their shareholders, who have reaped higher stock prices and dividends on the back of people who are sleeping in their cars.

In the dark days of 2012 and 2013, unique stories about a tech worker interning at Google and living in a box truck made the social media rounds. The exploitation of the American working class reaches into every industry.

One feature of modern work culture has been the literal evaporation of benefits. Most service industry jobs in retail, fast food, and food service don't offer benefits and keep their workers under the required hours to avoid paying for it. Even in middle-class office jobs, decent medical benefits can be hard to find or simply too expensive for the average person to afford.

Millennials have simply been left behind in the workforce. Fewer people are working, and they are making less money. "Since 2008, America has had a lower prime-age employment rate than any other G7 country except Italy." (Joey Politano via Twitter/X). This means economies like France (with its youth unemployment issue) and even the UK have been outperforming the U.S. in getting young people to work. This is the case because of the slow economic growth following the Great Financial Crisis.

In an article titled, "Let's Overshoot" by Matthew C. Klein, published on July 2, 2021, in his newsletter, The Overshoot, he remarked:

> The average American produced 2.2% more goods and services each year from the beginning of 1947 until the end of 2006. (According to the U.S. Bureau of Economic Analysis) Despite violent business cycles and countervailing forces, the U.S. economy stayed within 8% of its stable long-term trend until the financial crisis. The defining feature of the crisis wasn't the severity of the initial hit to incomes and production but what happened next: nothing. There was no snapback. There was no "Morning in America." The average American's real income didn't even return to its pre-crisis level until the middle of 2013. The agonizingly slow growth after the crisis meant that U.S. output per person by the eve of the Pandemic was 14%

below where it would have been if the 1946-2006 trend had held steady. It was an enormous and costly under-shoot. Put another way, the average American earned about $9,600 less in 2019 than would have been reasonably expected before the financial crisis.

An argument is often made that workers who are unsatisfied with their jobs or gig work should quit and get a better deal elsewhere. After all, they voluntarily chose to do this work at this price, right? The picture is not that simple. This argument assumes something every market researcher will say doesn't exist: perfect knowledge of a marketplace. This is especially true in employment, where the employer has far more expertise and holds more power than the employed person.

This argument assumes that the worker has time, inclination, and ability to exist without an income for as long as it takes to find that other job. This is not the reality for most workers, especially young workers. Also, not all workers have the same skills. A worker who has only worked in fast food may have trouble shifting to another industry with demonstrably better pay. This is particularly true in our modern economy. For white-collar workers, shift industries can be complex. Companies are often more likely to hire employees already in the same industry to reduce ramp-up time into a role. For other white-collar workers, it may be challenging to shift their skills to a different job if their current company or a new employer won't give them a chance. It is these unseen barriers that often prevent workers from simply getting a better deal.

Location is also a factor. There are only so many jobs in the area where a worker lives. Even if they are willing to commute long distances, jobs may not be available in other towns or cities within driving distance, making a costly move necessary. Many workers can't afford to move whenever they need a new job. Some industries are clustered in certain areas, and a change of location might denote a career change, which is a hard transition to make, especially with a family.

Many workers can't afford to be without an income long enough to find a new job, trapping them where they are while they seek other opportunities. They may not have the time and energy to pursue a different line of work after long hours. There are opportunity costs and the actual cost of retraining for something else. Platitudes about retraining or moving are thrown about casually when most people don't realize that many workers simply can't afford to do anything of the sort.

Deep within the American ethos is the idea that hard work will equal success. In the nineteenth century, titans of industry who seemingly came from nothing, like Andrew Mellon or Andrew Carnegie, were examples of people who could turn poverty into tremendous success. Millennials were taught that one could get ahead through hard work and dedication. However, it is difficult to work hard when no one will give you a chance to work hard to begin with. These considerations are what America's lost generation faced when they entered the job market in the anemic growth years after the recession. In *The Theft of a Decade* by Joseph Sternberg, he said of millennials entering the workforce during the recession, "Younger workers take up entry-level jobs with which to start building their skills, but many entry-level jobs often have a strong whiff of the routine or rote task about them. All in all, those routine jobs accounted for 94 percent of job losses during the recession."

Sternberg also shows that the situation continued to be dire through most of the last decade. The situation millennials have faced in the job market since 2009 has been adverse. "In October 2009, when the overall unemployment rate reached its Great Recession peak of 10 percent, the unemployment rate for people ages twenty-five to thirty-four (born 1975-1984), so the youngest Gen Xers and the oldest millennials, was 10.6 percent and the unemployment rate for the bulk of millennials then in the workforce (ages twenty to twenty-four, with birth years from 1985-1989 was 15.8 percent. Only in mid-2018, a decade after the Great Recession, did the unemployment rate for those ages twenty-five to -thirty-four approach parity with the unemployment rate for the overall labor force."

This dynamic covered the first decade of most millennials' working life, which meant trillions of wealth were lost by simply not being generated or flowing into the pockets of the wealthy. The number of people working has been affected as well. Sternberg goes on to state, "From a six percentage point gap in the 1990s when typically around 84 percent of older people were working compared to 78 percent of young twenty-somethings—the gap widened to nearer eight percentage points in the 2000s. And since the Great Recession, the gap has expanded to 11 percentage points."

Millennials who came out during these challenging times were faced with student loan debt and global workforce competition, often competing with their parents and older relatives for the same limited job opportunities. Instead of sending out twenty or thirty resumes and getting two or three interviews, millennials send out 400 or more resumes to get no interviews, much less a job offer. The picture was more rosy and regular in some fields like healthcare and tech. Outside of those fields, many millennials simply weren't getting hired.

Desperate for work, these bright young workers turned to retail and food service jobs. In the jobs that were created after the recession, our economy created millions of these sorts of jobs. For millennials who went to college, it was a step backward to the jobs they had worked in high school and college, only this time they would be trapped in those jobs for years with comparatively mediocre pay and a lifetime hit to their earnings. Unable to save, their lifetime wealth took a hit as well. Some have escaped those fields, while others still languish there.

Ten years later, the promise of education being a fast track to the middle class has left many millennials standing on the train platform, wondering if their train will ever arrive. It won't for many, and our current COVID-19 recession will only reinforce that, especially as those reliable service jobs have been decimated in a world where indoor dining has collapsed. Even Starbucks is closing stores to create better locations for social distancing and contactless pickups.

So the reality millennials face as we enter our early middle age is that we've inherited a fabulous job market—so long as we have in-demand skills and can get a job and get paid for it. However, even those fortunate to have the right combination of education, connections, job skills, interviewing skills, and ability to navigate the job market will likely be paid much less than their parents were at the same age. Sternberg reports, "The pay gap between older and younger workers is stark. Sternberg says, "One manifestation of this trend is a startling shift millennials have experienced acutely: it increasingly pays to be old. One study compared changes in median wages over time for men ages twenty-five and thirty-four and between forty-five and fifty-four. In contrast, older men tended to earn about 4 percent more than their younger counterparts in 1950, older men earned 11 percent more than younger men in 1970, and as of 2011 earned a whopping 41 percent more."

However, it is not merely these changes within the working world that have adversely affected millennials' careers. Bigger trends have also created unique situations within the American workforce that have all moved together like a great wave against millennials.

CHAPTER 13:

DIGITIZATION AND ADAPTATION

A submission from Reddit:

20 years old, High functioning Autism, born as the 90s closed and the 2000s dawned. My parents grew up fairly wealthy, not rich by any means, but wealthy enough to buy a suburban house in the middle of a street on a hill.

They had me and my brother, and they watched as their fortune faltered. In 08 they lost their jobs, in 16 my mom was hospitalized for a mental breakdown and resulted in me spending my last years of school in a mental state of nihilism and dreariness. I managed to survive school barely. And I cried when I did, believing in some hope in the world.

My job is, okay, I work hard in a grocery store and I try to keep my head down. The last year, it, broke me...Enough said...,enough done...Going to college? Why even bother? I will just be called a Libtard on the right, and suicidal on the left... I am only good at history, which won't give me a valid job, and I will be forced to live with my parents for...I don't even know how long...I might as well, just slit my wrist

> writing down the reasons for my death. But, I can't...I am
> a damn patriot for my country. I won't let the knife or the
> blade touch my skin. I am going to use the pen, and write till
> I can embrace death itself...

The working life of millennials has been a fraught one. Denied entry-level jobs and forced to come up with anything else in order to survive or thrive, the decade of Obama's nonrecovery and recovery made the first decade of millennials' working life a nightmare. The service industry expanded, but the wages were poor. The good jobs millennials thought their education would earn them were nowhere to be found. This has never really been fixed in any meaningful manner, and service industry jobs were often the first to go during the pandemic due to shutdowns of society. This has been a one-two punch for millennials. Work culture is deeply broken, and it has caused the latest trends of "quiet quitting," where people do only the work in their job description and nothing more, or the Chinese "lay flat" movement, where workers simply stop working altogether.

As Alice on Twitter/X said, "No one wants to work anymore because there is no reward. Half of us are living paycheck to paycheck. No saving for retirement. No saving for a house. Straight up two paychecks away from living on the street." This economic conundrum is backed up in *The Theft of a Decade*, too. Sternberg says of the lost generation, "Many Millennials have this surprising idea that not only should they have a job, but that job should pay enough to live within a reasonable distance from where they work, cover all their bills, and provide enough to save. This is not a revolutionary idea, but when millennials increasingly demand this, older people just shrug their shoulders and offer platitudes like, 'figure it out' or 'move somewhere cheaper.' Just figuring it out can take many forms. Although some have forgotten it, many millennials wrote gut-wrenching stories about living on ramen and rice while navigating inflated rents and low-paying work, even at America's best companies."

Another aspect of how the working lives and their economic future have been compromised comes from a series of trends that involve the gig economy, automation, and the failures of education policy in the United States.

GIG ECONOMY

The rise of the gig economy among the ashes of the 2008 financial crisis has affected almost every aspect of the American economy. Keeping people as independent contractors who can be hired on and let go as needed without any consideration beyond their material use to the means of production has infected almost every aspect of a business. Those of us who work in the arts are familiar with this, but now it has gone into tech, healthcare, and other industries where people used to enjoy a certain level of certainty and stability in their work.

From *The Theft of a Decade* again, "Global Temping firm ManpowerGroup surveyed a pool of millennials that included thousands of its temp-agency workers, a cohort who tend to be more precariously employed or underemployed relative to their level of education and skills. Those millennials' top workplace hopes and dreams? Money and job security."

Stability is difficult to find in a world where labor is seen as an interchangeable commodity like anything else. This is particularly pronounced in the rise of the gig economy apps. Uber, Lyft, DoorDash, Airbnb, GoPuff, and other such delivery/ride services cropped up after the recession, representing the growing trend in employment. Like other businesses, they offloaded their costs (cars, drivers, buildings) onto other people and made all the money by merely connecting a customer with a provider. They serve as the ultimate middle-man.

Initially, these were billed as something people would do as a side hustle to earn extra cash. However, ask any Uber driver, and they will tell you that they do it full-time, especially those who lease their cars through Uber and have to make enough money to survive and pay the lease on the vehicle. Such an arrangement is as bad as living in the company town. One false move could lose someone's whole livelihood. I was recently riding an Uber to pick up my car, and the driver told me that people were avoiding some areas of downtown Seattle because the cops would give them tickets if they picked anyone up from there. Apparently, I was lucky to get a ride. He reported that a driver can lose their car and be put off the app because of this.

This model of work has infected everything. Tech companies do it with their own workers. Nearly half of Google's workforce are contractors with no worker protections and few rights. Healthcare has also moved in this direction, with traveling nurses making far more than nurses employed by the hospital, and they can simply move on if a hospital doesn't work out for them.

The "gig" economy attitude is essentially breaking the economy. When workers do not have stability and certainty, buying a house or taking on any kind of debt is far more challenging. There is hardly any stability in life. Work might force a move to another location if you are not working remotely. This further devolves the stability of the community and family.

Nonetheless, this is now the modern standard. Workers are not part of a team or part of a company. They are merely another resource to be deployed, used, and disposed of as needed, like any other commodity.

Is it any surprise that rail workers in the fall of 2022 rebelled against precision railroading that gave them practically no time off and no time with their families and community? Is it a further surprise that Starbucks, Apple, and other businesses face unionization efforts like never before? Certainly not. Workers are tired of being treated as interchangeable pieces in a puzzle where they have no control, and the shifting nature of employment means they can be made homeless at any time by the whims of another. Indeed, this was the situation workers faced before the progressive labor movements of the 1920s and 1930s.

It took the death of several workers and general strikes to make the labor reforms commonplace today, like the weekend, an eight-hour work day, and other reforms. For gig workers, these advances have been rolled back. For other workers, the subsequent technological development, which will likely be more significant than the agricultural or industrial revolutions in both scope and depth, is automation.

AUTOMATION

Erik Brynjolfsson delivered this perfect encapsulation of the effects of automation on the economy in his article "The Turing Trap: The Promise & Peril of Human-Like Artificial Intelligence," published on January 11, 2022: "And it's starting to look like the big economic story of the past thirty years is that companies have been investing ever more heavily in technologies that replace labor and then make those labor-replacing technologies progressively more productive rather than investing primarily in technologies that augment labor."

Automation, which has already been a massive part of our lives, began with the computer revolution. Personal computers and all the devices that came with them started to displace workers in the 1990s. Add in other time-saving and labor-saving devices like the copy machine, and suddenly entry-level jobs were hollowed out. Before copy machines, there were typing pools and rooms full of people making duplicates of forms and documents. Then the computer came into the office and made managing the lives of professionals far easier, necessitating fewer people with secretaries. Now, thanks to the smartphone and the internet, people who previously would have needed a secretary or assistant can simply pick up their smartphone. *The Theft of a Decade* backs up my thesis on this topic where it states: "When people think about automation, they do not often think about all the ways tasks have been automated. Automation usually conjures images of large, expensive robots building cars. Automation also includes technology. For example, the copy machine pretty well killed off the secretarial pool. There was no need to have 30 people sitting at typewriters making copies of things using carbon paper when Xerox had a machine that could do it in moments. Keeping calendars digitally, emailing, and other advances have killed many clerical jobs. Most professionals perform their support work thanks to digital technology. Answering machines spelled the end of the answering service."

What has this meant for millennials? Nothing good or helpful. Between the effects of digitization and the computer and cost-cutting measures in the wake of the GFC, a whole class of entry-level jobs simply disappeared. This would define our early working years. Sternberg writes in *The Theft of a Decade*: "Millennials have faced the aftermath of these advancements. The entry-level jobs that once existed to help people climb the organizational ladder often don't exist. Many entry-level job postings ask for much more than would have been previously expected for young workers." This only compounds the problem addressed in the section Entry-Level Jobs. It was not simply that millennials would not take these jobs—they didn't exist in the first place. With automation killing off these jobs, job growth had to take place elsewhere, and it took place in the service industry. The millennials' trope is a younger person who went to college, got an excellent education at a terrible expense, and now works at Starbucks. We can see from the real-life stories contained in these pages that this has undoubtedly been the case for some folks. Part of the failure of the job market has to do with automation. When the simple and routine jobs get automated away, experience in doing something that is neither simple nor routine begins to matter greatly.

EDUCATION

A submission from Reddit:

> Long story really, probably also a common one. Childhood trauma: one parent was a narcissist the other was a somewhat

emotionally distant workaholic both had boomer ideology. Grew up in a miserable upper middle class life, can't even hack lower middle class myself. Then when I went to college I was overwhelmed with stress my parent didn't seem to approve of me not wanting to do stem/medical/legal so I just felt so trapped and controlled I ended up on SSRIs which gave me bad side effects including worsened depression and then everything spiraled into free fall after that, ended up with PTSD from an emotionally abusive doctor and haven't been able to get my body to function on an 8-5 office grind really ever. Boomers seem to be very ableist and wouldn't flex my schedule enough so my body kind of collapsed after a while trying to hold the jobs down. Mainly when I think about boomers I think they caused their children's disabilities through trauma and then we end up in the medical industrial rabbit hole that won't name the problem.

I was labeled gifted as a child. I always tested in the top 5% usually the top 1-2% I am burned out and recovering slowly from chronic physical handicap and PTSD as an adult. Renter all my life and never owned a car. Still get advice that's meant well but has no basis in reality from boomers like "just get more credentials/schooling" and suffered due to their workplace rules like having to bench-warm 8-5 even though it would be so easy to do most from home.

The non-narcissist parent has improved immensely in their relational efforts but growing up it was very much boomer ideology nonstop.

Sorry above when I meant name the problem I mean a lot of us just really mentally collapsed under the pressure of their ideology. When I went to college at 18 on a full ride for academic achievement I didn't know what I wanted to do. I felt like "a career" was paramount.

I got a retail job for 9.75 an hour in Bellevue Washington, after graduating with 2 years research assistant exp, 6 months mental health call center and 6 months teaching assistant. My boomer parent wanted me to get a job by a certain date after graduation and that's the only concrete offer on the table by the deadline.

My degree is in psychology. My intended career was research assistant/study coordinator. So many times I see that the world is like inhospitable soil now; there is nowhere to put down roots. No job that will keep you 20 years from a firm handshake and a connection, no housing that is sustainable or attainable. We're all just drifting and skating by. Security feels like a fantasy.

RACE TO THE TOP AND NO CHILD LEFT BEHIND

No two pieces of legislation have changed the American educational landscape like No Child Left Behind (NCLB), passed by the Bush administration, and Race to the Top, passed by the Obama administration to replace NCLB. Rather than moving away from standardized testing, as other countries have done, the NCLB tied standardized test scores to funding. This had a profound and deleterious effect on the American education system. Instead of learning subjects and developing skills and mastery, students learned how to pass a test. Any program that couldn't be easily measured on a test often saw the chopping block. Instead of fixing the achievement gap, in many cases both of these programs made the problem worse. One goal of the program was to prepare students for college. This was a goal for underperforming schools and schools where minority students were predominant. These changes had the greatest effect on Gen Z, but late cohort millennials saw the beginnings of these changes. This education policy impacted students, but it was the narrative about educational attainment that would be most poisonous to millennials: college.

The narrative was pervasive in the 90s and aughts. To be successful, young people had to go to college. High school guidance counselors preached this idea. Student debt was deemed "good debt" by financial gurus like Suze Orman and others. The theory went that the earnings achieved with a college degree ($1 million additional dollars earned, a statistic often quoted from the federal government) would make the debt worth it. However, this was predicated on the availability of jobs for freshly minted college graduates.

Politicians were in the game, too. They touted their success in education by raising test scores and more kids going to college than ever before. Voters loved this as it fulfilled the American dream: doing better than your parents. Many students were the first in their families to go to college. Parents encouraged kids to go to college. Still other parents demanded it of their children. Much like the person in the story at the beginning of this chapter, college was not an option for many students. It was an edict from parents to young people who had long grown used to following along with what their parents wanted.

THE PROBLEM WITH COLLEGE

Institutions that have come under scrutiny since the Great Financial Crisis are colleges and universities. As we know, millennials are the most educated generation in American history. Millennials went to college in droves, hoping to secure a position in the middle class or move up socially into a new class. For many, this upward leap was a disaster.

H. Bruce Franklin, in an August 31, 2022, article titled "Why Talk about Loans?" in the online magazine *CounterPunch*, talked about the genesis of the current crisis in higher education. He wrote, "Later in 1970, Roger Freeman—a key educational adviser to Nixon then working for the reelection of California governor Ronald Reagan—spelled out quite precisely what the conservative counterattack was aimed at preventing: 'We are in danger of producing an educated proletariat. That's dynamite! We have to be selective on who we allow to go through higher education. If not, we will have a large number of highly trained and unemployed people.'"

As much as we might not want to hear it, Roger Freeman was probably not incorrect on that score. Indeed, that is what millennials have become: an educated proletariat. This also goes along with a recent canard about the over production of elites. This argument has been made by people like Noah Smith on Twitter/X, but it has also reached the pages of *The Economist*. The argument goes that too many elites lead to revolution and economic problems. Too many educated people can only lead to problems. When it comes to millennial complaints about the economy and the changes being forced up from below, they probably weren't incorrect.

These dynamics have not stopped higher education from becoming a pathway to the middle class but only within the right major. Growing up, millennials were often told (as I was) that the major didn't matter but that I had gone to college at all. I could major in whatever I liked. I chose a field of interest where I already had some experience and thought I was putting myself on an excellent pathway to being hired straight out of school. The Great Financial Crisis completely changed the game; overnight, whole colleges and universities became unmarketable. I used to rent from a lady who is an award-winning actress and now works in Public Health. Her major in college? Comparative literature. That is the way it used to be. The standard changed, and anyone in the humanities suddenly found themselves out in the cold, being passed by business majors and STEM majors. Tech absorbed all these people and paid them obscene amounts of money in the years after the GFC. If you made the mistake of majoring in the humanities, Starbucks was hiring.

In these discussions, the humanities have become the poster child of failed experiments in education. One annoying person on Twitter/X commented back at me, "90% of humanities grads haven't read three great works of literature in their entirety, don't understand the concept of a demand curve, and couldn't tell you what a derivative is. BS'ing term papers on analytic philosophy, Chinese politics, and Russian literature isn't an education."

In *Guernica*, Matt Burriesci wrote:

> What role will the arts and humanities play in this brave new world? We cannot measure the value of these disciplines in dollars, so we have decided that they have no value at all except some token value, like the parsley garnish on a 16-ounce steak. They're nice but not really necessary, and certainly not as necessary as STEM. We don't need more historians, philosophers, and artists; we need students who know how to code, how to write concise business memoranda, and, most ominously, how to answer all our questions. I suspect that many on the political right would agree with President Obama's glib remark about the value of art history: "I promise you folks can make a lot more, potentially, with skilled manufacturing or the trades than they might with an art history degree." The president later apologized, of course. Yet it's clear that President Barack Obama (an author, orator, and constitutional law professor) believes that the nation would be better off if our citizens engaged less with art, history, rhetoric, and philosophy, and engaged more with plumbing, engineering, and software design.

That is certainly the prevailing attitude, and given the poor performance of his economy, President Obama was merely espousing the conventional wisdom of his presidency. His remarks aligned with every Reddit comment posted in the last decade that encouraged anyone with a humanities degree to either learn to code or die.

Mr. Burriesci finished the article by saying:

> More than three centuries ago, a generation of philosophers, political thinkers, economic geniuses, and scientists created

our way of life. It's no coincidence that this singular political achievement coincided with the dawn of the Industrial Revolution. All the prosperity we now enjoy (and all we have enjoyed since the dawn of our republic) is owed entirely to thinkers who understood the inestimable value of philosophy, history, and the arts. How do you measure the value of liberalism, capitalism, or the American State Papers? I don't know, except to suggest that if we did it in dollars, the cumulative GDP of the United States since its inception would be an extremely conservative starting point. But that is a silly exercise, similar to assessing the value of the Parthenon by measuring its square footage and proximity to major highways. The value of the arts and humanities has nothing to do with money. It is that same value Socrates identified with the Athenians before he was put to death for heresy and corrupting the youth: the value of knowing that we do not know. It is the value of answering incorrectly and challenging the culture and its conventional wisdom. It is the courage to say, 'We cannot go on as we have. We must change. We need a new operating system.'

The primary trouble with the humanities is that they tend to lead to low-wage jobs that do not fulfill the upwardly mobile desires of students or their parents. No jobs are available for "can create a new paradigm for society." Also, many students have to borrow money for the privilege of higher education. If the $1.7 trillion dollar student loan crisis has taught us anything, there must be a financial consideration for college. Someone has to pay all that money back, and if a degree doesn't directly lead to a job, and a good-paying one at that, then the degree is virtually pointless. As someone with three degrees in the humanities, it hurts my soul to read about this, but given my own resume, I can't say that it's an incorrect statement. This shift in attitude has led to a change within higher education. Over the past decade, this has led to colleges and universities cutting already sparse funding from the humanities departments. Some departments have been eliminated, while others are watching enrollment dwindle.

The *National Review* reported in 2018, in an article titled "The Liberal Arts Weren't Murdered – They Committed Suicide," that "Recently the University of Wisconsin – Stevens Point announced plans to drop liberal arts majors in geography, geology, French, German, two- and three-dimensional art—and history." *The Atlantic* ran an insightful essay by Adam Harris titled, "The Liberal Arts May Not Survive the 21st Century." Harris argues that the insidious efforts to promote STEM education—driven by a perceived need to prepare young people for careers in science, technology, engineering, and math—has marginalized the liberal arts. This trend is exacerbated by severe budget cuts to public higher education in several states, often pushed by crass Republican state legislators, in an allegedly vindictive and short-sighted fashion, which has further undermined the viability of liberal arts programs.

The Stevens Point campus highlighted a widespread perception that emphasis on literature, history, or languages lead nowhere for cash-strapped graduates but to more debt and fewer jobs. Yet the article on official university policy misses why students do not concentrate on the liberal arts in the fashion of the past.

The sad reality is that the 2008 crisis changed the game regarding which college majors were in demand and which were not. One of the darkest moments of my collegiate career was getting dressed up, resumes in hand, and walking over to my school's job fair. I stepped into the midcentury modern University Center toward the big ballrooms only to be turned away because the recruiters inside were only interested in business majors and the like. When I said I was majoring in political science, they acted like it was a disease that they might catch. I was turned away from the fair. The rules had changed, and I had been studying a subject I enjoyed and thought would earn me a good position. I was naive to the changes going on around me.

Justin Stover, himself a professor at Oxford and the University of Edinburgh, writing for *American Affairs Journal*, was quoted in the magazine *Pacific Standard* saying, "It's just that now, as universities become corporate boot camps churning out productive science, technology, engineering, mathematics (STEM) students, the humanities can no longer compete under the new rules. To try to do so is to engage in self-defeat. The justification for the humanities only makes sense within a humanistic framework. Outside of it, there is simply no case."

For both institutions and universities, the humanities are a tricky thing. They do lend some cachet, but the students participating may have trouble finding a job afterward. As is the case for many people whose stories I recount in this book, they end up in low-wage, service jobs that they could have gotten without the associated debt from their degrees that the American economy has decided, in its great wisdom, are useless.

Stover is quoted again in the *Pacific Standard*: "The most prestigious universities in the West are still those defined by their humanities legacy, which surrounds them with an aura of cultural standing that their professional purpose no longer justifies. The humanities continue to lend cachet to educational credentials, granting an elite status worth far more than any 'marketable skills.' That is why every technical institute with higher aspirations has added humanities programs: Accounting, law, or engineering can be learned in many places, but courtliness is passed along only in the university and through the humanities—and everyone knows it."

Does elite status matter if the best a humanities major can do is serve coffee at Starbucks? Because of this, enrollments are way down, even before the pandemic and the Great Financial Crisis.

The article "The Humanities Are Dead. Long Live the Humanities" by James McWilliams in the *Pacific Standard* (where he also quotes Justin Stover) states:

As of 2015, only 12 percent of undergraduates at colleges and universities in the U.S. graduated with a degree in the humanities. A 2017 analysis of the changing concentrations of Harvard University sophomores found alarming declines in the humanities. It also found a corresponding rise in STEM disciplines. Between 2008 and 2016, history majors went from 231 to 136; English majors went from 236 to 144; art history majors went from 63 to 36; anthropology majors went from 126 to 43; comparative literature majors went from 48 to 16; and classics majors went from 41 to 26. By contrast, applied mathematics went from 101 to 279; electrical engineering went from 0 to 39; computer science went from 85 to 386; and statistics went from 17 to 173. These numbers mirror national trends. In my own discipline, history, majors have dropped by 25 percent between 2001 and 2016, a figure made especially alarming by the fact that it's a decline from 2.08 percent to 1.54 percent of all undergraduate degrees. In 1970, it was close to 6 percent. At my own university, it's around 1 percent.

McWilliams goes on to argue that the humanities will live on but that they might live on outside the institutions of higher learning, at least in the United States, and that podcasts and other digital mediums can do an excellent job of relating the principles of Emerson, Thoreau, Virgil, and Horace to people who are interested in that sort of thing. While this is undoubtedly good news for The Cameron Journal Podcast, I know I could not do what I do without my educational background. There is a difference between being merely well read and educated.

However, not all hope is lost. In the intervening years when this discourse has gone on from time to time, the value of the humanities has had a bit of a renaissance. *Inc. Magazine* reported in 2019: "The bottom line is that, if you're inclined more towards the humanities than the likes of computer science, then a good liberal arts degree will help you do well in your career and is generally well worth the time and money it takes to earn. 'All the evidence shows that the bashing of liberal arts colleges, and the liberal arts, just isn't well founded, just isn't based on evidence,' concludes author Catharine B. Hill."

With the rise of AI and other technologies that promise to automate many tasks, including those done by STEM majors, having flexible skills from the humanities can make people more resilient in their long-term careers. However, given the financial troubles, the argument for the humanities is a tough one. When it comes to higher education, for most Americans, it does come down to return on investment.

STUDENT LOANS

One of the most contentious things many millennials have faced as America's most educated generation is the student loan crisis. This crisis begins with two separate situations.

The first aspect of the student loan crisis is that millennials, mainly working class and middle class millennials, were sold the concept that going to college was the fastest way to advancement in society. The script was clear: go to college and get a good job. Millions of millennials followed this path. For those from less fortunate circumstances, student debt was seen as a necessity. Financial gurus billed student debt as so-called "good debt," the theory being that the result of a spike in earnings from getting a degree would offset the upfront expense of the loans.

The other aspect of this crisis was how the United States decided to fund or defund higher education in this country. Student loans are essentially a tax on the upwardly mobile. Rather than have society pay for the costs and benefits of higher education, the burden of funding America's institutions of higher learning ends up being borne by the people who go to them. Many people had forgotten that New York University and two California university systems were essentially free until the 1980s when their respective states pulled funding. This happened throughout the country. Politicians heralded it as a way to save taxpayer money, but what the politicians didn't tell the people was that it would be much more expensive for their kids to go to college if they weren't already coming from a place of economic privilege.

Since then, the cost of going to college has skyrocketed. According to *Forbes*, "In 1980, the price to attend a four-year college full-time was $10,231 annually—including tuition, fees, room and board, and adjusted for inflation—according to the National Center for Education Statistics. By 2019-20, the total price had increased to $28,775. That's a 180% increase."

Sternberg remarks on student loan programs and student loan forgiveness from the Obama administration. "Worse, note who would ultimately foot the bill for all this debt forgiveness. Not just taxpayers but a certain kind of taxpayer: Millennial taxpayers. The time horizons for these programs mean that the taxpayer bills will only start coming due around 2027 at the earliest. Who will be working and paying taxes by then? Not the Baby Boom generation. The youngest Boomers born in 1964 will all have reached age sixty-seven and retirement by 2031, and most of them will be long gone from the labor force before then. President Obama's big show of generosity towards millennial students amounted to forcing us to make a gift to ourselves. Oh, and then Washington would take some of it away again by taxing any remaining loan amount that's forgiven as 'income.'"

Even despite President Biden's program to do the same, it will cost upwards of $500 billion, and the people who will be paying the most are millennials themselves, especially as they move into the tax-paying class over the next five to ten years.

The mantra fed to most middle-class and upper-class millennials was that to be successful, they needed to go to college, and they did so, becoming the most educated generation in American history. However, it did not pay off for many. Student debt was problematic enough, but on top of that, the needed on-the-job training and early entry-level jobs were simply not available, making their education seem useless. Many of the rote and routine tasks that were stepping stones to further promotion had been eliminated—or automated away—largely due to advances in technology.

In the wake of these economic changes, suddenly, it seemed like anyone who had gone to college was a dupe, and all the real wage action was in trade schools and vocational schools. In the multi-year dialogue that has been going on about millennials and their failure to launch, people in social media comment sections will quip that people "should have gone to trade school" and avoided "getting degrees in nothing." Mike Rowe, the host of the famous "Dirty Jobs" television show, has been a large voice in this discussion, even though he is college-educated.

Millennials faced a difficult situation where they needed entry-level jobs, but none were offered, and jobs kept raising the requirements. In *The Theft of a Decade*, Sternberg wrote, "A Major study of online job postings found that in metropolitan areas hit hardest by recessions, the number of job ads requiring a minimum level of prior experience increased, to 52 percent from 32 percent. Although most of that increase came from employers seeking between zero and three years of experience (to 24 percent from 13 percent), this still signals that employers felt they could expect applicants to walk in the door with some prior experience already."

This trend in job postings devastated millennials coming out of college and into the workforce between 2009 and 2013. Not much has changed in the intervening years. Many job postings will go viral on social media due to asking for high experience and low pay only since the pandemic has wages begun to grow at any appreciable amount. However, thanks to inflation, real wages are still falling. Employees have the power to change jobs, get more money, and sell their skills at a faster rate than at any time in decades. For millennials, the post-pandemic job market is the most advantageous they've ever seen.

Sternberg goes on to say:

> This approach helps to explain several important phenom-
> ena that have been become crucial for millennials. First,
> since the recession of the early 1990s these lost routine
> jobs haven't come back during economic recoveries. Rou-
> tine jobs kept disappearing even after the Great Recession
> formally ended: another 2.3 percent were lost in the two
> years after the American economy tipped back into positive
> growth in 2009. And second, this form of jobless recov-
> ery"—an economic rebound in which continuing losses of
> routine jobs prevent the total number of jobs created from
> rising appreciably—reached full flower just as millennials
> started entering the workforce…. Comparing this figure
> (actual jobs created) to what economists know about the
> different tendencies of different age groups to change jobs,
> by one count millennial young adults account for two-thirds
> of the short fall between actual job creation after the Great
> Recession and the jobs that would have been created if the
> economy and continued growing at the same pace as before.
> Put another way, millennials between 2009 and 2013 missed
> out on some fifty-five million job opportunities they other-
> wise might have been able to hop between on their path to
> a stable career.

The Great Financial Crisis deprived millennials of the jobs they
needed to get their careers off the ground. That is one part of the
story. The other part of the story is how the economy changed
between 1995 and 2008. The reality is that many trade deals and the
onset of globalization had hollowed out the American middle class
and left families wondering what would happen to them. This narrative
made it into popular media of the time.

In Season 5, Episode 19 of *The West Wing,* the iconic Aaron Sorkin show, trade comes front and center. In the story, Josh Lyman negotiates another new trade deal hailed as a way forward for trade and new American jobs. A family enters his office to know why he is signing away the husband's job.

He admits that it will create more jobs in the long term, but that short-term pain was the price. The husband remarks that he has recently changed jobs four times, trying to keep up with this new economy. He plaintively asked what the government was going to do about it. As Josh Lyman, Bradley Whitford delivered this iconic line that expresses the thinking of the time, "We're going to do what we can to prepare you; we have to." This was a standard narrative as a raft of new trade deals were signed in the 1990s and early 2000s, including the North America Free Trade Agreement (NAFTA) that was recently renegotiated by President Trump in 2018, and the most favored nation trading status for China in 2000 through the World Trade Organization (WTO). When the WTO held its meeting in Seattle in 1999, riots broke out over labor protections and child labor.

In the 1990s and early 2000s, several new trade deals that would form an international structure for globalization had been signed into law. Offshoring and moving jobs overseas would pick up pace. In 2012, the Information Technology and Innovation Foundation published a report that said, "In the 2000s, U.S. manufacturing suffered its worst performance in American history in terms of jobs. Not only did America lose 5.7 million manufacturing jobs, but the decline as a share of total manufacturing jobs (33 percent) exceeded the loss rate in the Great Depression. Despite this unprecedented negative performance, most economists, pundits, and elected officials are remarkably blasé about what has transpired. Manufacturing, they argue, has simply become incredibly productive. While tough on laid-off workers, job losses indicate superior performance. All that is needed, if anything, are better programs to help laid-off workers."

That represented a gutting of the basis of the American economy. Fortunately, the economy was growing in a variety of other ways. While a late cohort of Gen X would be disadvantaged from the 1999-2002 recession that was a combination of the dotcom bubble burst and the events of September 11, 2001, they bounced back in a few short years and were better prepared for what was to come. Although the story of globalization and trade was in focus enough at the time to make it into an award-winning television show, the story of international trade had begun decades earlier.

After World War II, the United States was one of the few wealthy countries whose entire economy and manufacturing base hadn't been destroyed by war. By 1945, the only two players left standing were the U.S. and the Soviet Union. The Soviet Union had to push back a disastrous German invasion, and the Soviet economy was notoriously inefficient due to central planning. The Cold War would soon leave the Soviets out of the global trading order anyway.

The post-war economic environment allowed the U.S. to replace the UK as the center of political and financial power. The dollar replaced the pound as the world's reserve currency, and in a famous meeting in New Hampshire, the Bretton Woods agreement was created to govern international trade. That agreement would peg the price of gold and the value of the dollar at 35:1, or 35 U.S. dollars, for every ounce of gold. This created the gold standard for the U.S. currency until Nixon ended the Bretton Woods system in 1971. The Bretton Woods system allowed the U.S. to be the net importer of goods and run trade deficits with its trading partners in Europe and Japan, giving them a chance to rebuild their economies on an export basis. The U.S. surplus was such that the rest of the world absorbed it to their benefit, and all global trade would now take place in dollars.

After 1971, the Bretton Woods system was reformed in a treaty called the General Agreement on Trade and Tariffs (GATT). These rules would govern global trade until GATT was subsumed and formed the basis of the World Trade Organization. Any nation that has signed onto the WTO must abide by its tariff rules, which included having the same tariffs for all trading partners and resolving trading disputes through the WTO. As President Trump reviewed the trading regime of the United States, everyone became familiar with the WTO and its various rules.

Free trade has various benefits, but it has some downsides, too. There is no way within WTO to protect domestic industries and save them from foreign competition. Free trade agreements allow both sides to sell to each other on ideal terms with the least trade barriers and the lowest tariffs. American manufacturers were thirsty to get into the growing Chinese market. Still, the lower cost of labor and lower costs of Chinese goods often left American manufacturers out in the cold. Manufacturing jobs bled out of the American Midwest as more companies either closed because they could not compete or moved jobs to China, where labor costs were lower despite rules in China that companies had to have a Chinese partner firm that owned 51 percent of the operation.

The decline in manufacturing jobs has contributed to a hollowing out of the American economy. Since new information and technology jobs were created, these jobs have primarily been for highly educated people in coastal cities. Kodak, at its height, employed 145,000 people; when Facebook bought Instagram, the whole company employed only 14 people. San Francisco has done well. Pittsburgh has not done so well. In this example between Kodak and Instagram, it is easy to point out that Kodak missed the advent of digital photography (despite owning the technology behind it) and foolishly focused on its legacy film business. The greater point is that all our modern tech and apps are convenient and have changed our lives, but the reality is that this technology does not create as many jobs as the old economy did. Technology was essentially deflationary as well. Money moved through the economy less quickly because wealth was concentrated in ever-fewer hands.

This has left far fewer positions for American millennials, especially non-educated workers, to take on to begin their careers. Even for educated millennials, there are two industries where good job demand is high: technology and healthcare. A good job is hard to find for those who could not enter those fields or whose interest, expertise, and talent might lie elsewhere.

American millennials aren't the only ones struggling either. The austerity politics of the United Kingdom in the years after the Great Financial Crisis have left many people without career options. Faced with high rents in London and in an economy where London has systematically sucked up all the economic growth, young people have been living in worse conditions than San Francisco tech bros to get by. Some just had to give up. Various governments attempted to improve the situation for young people in the UK. The living wage increase (2015) to seven pounds fifty was a step forward. However, this has been undermined by an assiduous reduction in the social safety net under years of Tory governments. This has left young people without connections or existing familial wealth out in the cold in the UK, where there are fewer opportunities than in previous years.

Across Europe, youth unemployment continues to be stubbornly high. France boasts a 22 percent unemployment rate (pre-pandemic), and for many young people in Spain and Italy, it is simply better to move abroad to get their career off the ground. Countries like Ireland and Greece have long exported their people to growing economies. It has often been said that Ireland's greatest export was her people. This trend continues across the continent.

CHAPTER 14:

NEETs

In my 20s, I was a bit of an outlier. I had gotten my master's degree at 23, and I had always had a job of some sort. However, by that time, the Great Financial Crisis happened, and despite riding out most of it in school, I found myself freshly graduated with few prospects. It was even worse for those who hadn't gone to school. Many young people found themselves back at home thanks to a lackluster job market, low wages, and rising housing costs. I was also in the same boat. In 2011, faced with no job prospects, the advice not to go to law school, and little interest in PhD programs, I moved back in with my parents.

In 2012, according to Pew Research, "Among the three-in-ten young adults ages 25 to 34 (29%) who've been in that situation during the rough economy of recent years, large majorities say they're satisfied with their living arrangements (78%) and upbeat about their future finances (77%)." However, not everything was precisely rosy about the situation. "To be sure, most young adults who find themselves under the same roof with mom and dad aren't exactly living the high life. Nearly eight-in-ten (78%) of these 25- to 34-year-olds say they don't currently have enough money to lead the kind of life they want, compared with 55% of their same-aged peers who aren't living with their parents. Even so, the large majority of both groups (77% versus 90%) say they either have enough money now to lead the kind of life they want or expect they will in the future."

The NEET phenomenon, Not in Education, Employment, or Training, is the moniker for people, usually young and male individuals, who simply exist. Much like the Japanese *hikikomori*, these young people who find themselves in this lifestyle often see no way to get out. They are frequently lost in the limbo of life. The only jobs available after high school without education are usually in the service industry or retail. It is important to note that in the decade since the Pew Research report about millennials, Gen Z has followed a similar pattern and has taken to the NEET lifestyle even more than their millennial siblings and cousins. At this point, the oldest millennials are in their 40s, with the youngest having just turned 30. This phenomenon is now a part of American adulthood as we know it.

Although it's not the result of the NEET phenomenon, the number of young people living at home has grown substantially since 2008. In his book *Not Working, Where Have All the Good Jobs Gone?*, Blanchflower writes in chapters two and three about how young people not moving out harms them and the economy. In reality, young people who are not moving forward in life end up stuck, often with no natural way out of the situation.

The service and retail industry jobs often don't pay enough for young people to live on their own, much less start relationships and families. This phenomenon affected millennials profoundly, and Gen Z has stayed at home and become NEETs in even higher numbers. The trope of millennials and other young people (who are no longer young) living in their parents' basement forever and complaining about society exists for a reason. However, there is an economic story here as well. Just as *hikikomori* get left behind in Japanese society once they drop out, many young people who drop out of society to become NEETs don't seem to have an on-ramp either.

NEETs tend to be overwhelmingly male, like their Japanese counterparts. This coincides with a steady decrease in prime-age male employment. In his book *Men Without Work: Post-Pandemic Edition*, Dr. Nicholas Eberstadt shows how the employment of prime-age men (ages 25 to 54) has been in steady decline since World War II, with a few big drops in the early 1980s (around 1982 during a recession) and then a major draw down after 2008. He reports that we are missing about ten million men in the workforce. In my book *What The Hell is Going on?*, I wrote a piece on this very subject, based on an article in *The Atlantic*. The question is, where did they go?

Blanchflower goes on to write: "They had been left behind this long drift where the less educated, in particular, were being delighted. It had been going on for years but was exacerbated by the Great Recession. For example, free trade benefited most people in the United States through lower prices, but the winners didn't adequately compensate the losers who spoke up. The good jobs went away to China and the Far East, but the big city elites did just fine. Immigrants became the obvious targets of people's anger and frustration. Illegal immigrants lowered the price of food, gardening, and childcare, for example, but workers at the low end felt they were taking their jobs away. Similarly, these folks voted for Brexit in the UK and Le Pen in France."

Dr. Nicholas Eberstadt has noted that for every unemployed American man between the ages of 25 and 55, there are another three who are not looking for work. He colorfully concludes that the unemployment rate "increasingly looks like an antique index devised from some earlier and increasingly distant war: the economic equivalent of a musket inventory or a calvary count."

Some men are in the gray economy doing odd jobs, usually paid in cash. The gray economy disappeared during the pandemic as businesses were forced to close for the first time in American history. While some can work for the family, others can be found simply at home without independence or money. Mental health issues like depression and anxiety often abound.

I met a few of these guys in 2017 while playing many video games after work. The daily life of a NEET isn't quite as secluded as the Japanese *hikikomori*. Still, similar habits can be found, like being online chronically, playing video games for hours, and relying on parents for basic needs.

Interestingly, this phenomenon, while overwhelmingly male, is not exclusively male. That being said, women are outpacing men by nearly every metric. Although it is often talked about in the present, women have been the majority of college graduates since the early 2000s. Black women have made significant gains in college education and are now one of the most educated groups in the country. Women represent about sixty-five percent of college graduates (2022), and that trend is holding steady. It has become enough of a crisis to garner media attention from pundits like Scott Galloway.

If you visit r/NEET on Reddit, you can observe the macabre parade of young people looking outside, much like their Japanese cousins decide to turn inward. Their posts are a masterclass in depression, hopelessness, and anger. There are strategies to remain a NEET, make money, get on disability, and mooch off family members. An undercurrent makes fun of those who work for a wage. They are called "wage slaves" or "wages" in the parlance of the community.

These attitudes could have two parts: self-hatred from not having what they ultimately want, and genuinely rejecting the modern economic system. Criticism of the monetary system grows out of this attitude. Posts about working for money that isn't worth anything and can be printed at will can be found. Still others reject how modern life slots people into a nine-to-five schedule and dominates their time—time they would rather spend doing something else.

Playing video games as a pastime is very common. Most NEET individuals live with a family member. Others reported doing well in school but, at some point, fell off that path and suddenly had no idea what to do with themselves. Many look down on the low-wage work that is so common today and often see this kind of work as simply not worthwhile. Why get out of bed to make a minimum wage that is unlivable when it seems just as easy to stay in bed if someone continues to make sure a bed exists? One sad poster reported that his "NEETdom" ended because his family was poor and he simply had to work.

Many people might look at these people as the ultimate losers, but underneath all the "wagecuckery" comments is a passion for life that is quite admirable. While some posters would like to lie in bed and stare at a wall, many, much like their Japanese counterparts, have passions and things that they love and would rather be doing, hence their seeming rejection of work.

Most people identifying as NEETs weren't directly affected by the 2008 crisis. Much like their Japanese counterparts, they were caught up in the aftermath of the cultural shifts that happen when it seems like the world is falling apart. In America, NEETs are the legacy of an economy that has left many behind. Wages have been stagnant for so long that working does not seem worthwhile for many. When a job cannot pay someone enough to live their life, what is the point of work? This is the logic of the NEET.

Much like their Japanese counterparts, society has soundly rejected them. The fact is that someone with only a high school diploma has limited life opportunities. The only escape is either through college or the trades. Much like the Japanese, a government program to help NEETs rejoin society could be helpful. Japanese society must bend to accept those who are different. While not as traditional as the Japanese, American society needs to create an environment where work pays off and people, especially young people, can feel like they will move forward with their lives. Many NEETs could be cured with a job that offered a decent wage, dignity, and a certain amount of freedom to pursue their passions. We used to call that the American dream.

SECTION 4:

MONEY, POLITICS, AND LIFE

Money is the one problem that millennials have never been able to solve. Quite simply, millennials just don't have enough of it. Millennials control only four percent of the nation's wealth. Older generations hold the rest of the wealth. Housing costs have prevented many from buying a home and building wealth in this manner. The high cost of rent has assiduously sucked money from the pockets of millennials into the pockets of those lucky enough to own property already. The lack of wage growth has hit millennials particularly hard. Also, the loss of earnings during the earliest part of their careers has not helped their pocketbooks. However, if you had told most millennials or their parents in 2006 that this would be the case, everyone would have laughed in your face. After all, millennials did everything society demanded of them. They stayed in school, did fewer drugs than their Gen X cousins, and got good grades. Millennials crowded into colleges, making them the most educated generation in American history. And yet, all that progress, education, and hard work has not paid off for the vast majority of the cohort, especially for those from modest, working-class backgrounds with aspirations of mobility. Even for kids from upper-class backgrounds, the downward mobility was unexpected. Many younger home buyers rely on their parents to help them get on the property ladder. It wasn't supposed to work this way. What happened?

CHAPTER 15:

THE GREAT MILLENNIAL MYTH

A submission from Reddit:

> I earned an undergrad business degree from a CA college in 2009. The sense that there is a corporate ladder to climb up is gone. Either I somehow entrepreneur myself a new ladder with extreme work and even more extreme luck, or I'm stuck hopping from one insular opportunity to another.
>
> Opportunities don't at all seem to lead to new opportunities anymore. Gone are the days of being hired, doing a good job, and getting a wage increase. It's a fight for employment, I should feel "grateful" whenever I am employed regardless of the workload/wage discrepancy, and if I have any hope of advancing I need to interview and jump to another company.

Another submission from Reddit:

> 30yr old woman with a bio BA from a well-known college who got stuck working in sales. I find it really funny now that I majored in bio with the intention to never work an office

job but found myself working in an office because I was desperate for a full-time stable job at 25 never having had one. The people I went to school with who were most successful after college were the ones with family connections to get them stable jobs after school. For years I compared myself to them and felt like such a failure. They're supposed to be my equals right? We all got into the same school right? I realized my nearly 80% scholarship was nothing but a pair of golden handcuffs when I was so depressed my first year I needed to take leave, though I couldn't afford to lose any money and my family couldn't provide me with a safe place to stay and get my head together. In a lot of different ways I still feel like I'm still recovering from everything I did in 2008 just to pay for/get into college. Including a pageant that nearly induced an eating disorder and subjected me to bullying from my entire high school.

Once I entered the job market as essentially (my father has a nursing degree from the Philippines where education is very different) a first-generation college grad I didn't know that my biology BA might as well be toilet paper as far as getting into lab work. No one ever told me that it was essential to get experience from working with a professor. And when I did try to get advice from a prof right before graduation I was mostly told to worry more about making time for having kids from a male prof I admired. The sexism didn't end there, I was told secretly that since bio is such a female-saturated field that I was denied a position at a well-known biotech firm because there were already too many women in the lab. A friend told me that to make me feel better, instead, it made me give up on bio. I felt like I couldn't win and all I wanted was an entry-level position doing PCR, a job which essentially does not need the knowledge of a four-year degree to do. Even worse was the realization that using my full first name on my resume was prejudicing hiring managers from even giving me a call. Once I changed my resume, I started finally getting calls back and realizing that racism inherent in the system made me feel even more like I'd been lied to. In a lot of ways it broke my heart.

By sucking up to people at enough alumni happy hours, I finally made a connection to get a good office job. It was publishing sales and it was supposed to just be for a little while so I could finally move out of my parents' house and think about grad school. Instead, I stayed for years while trying to pay for medical procedures I needed and were not covered by insurance. My medical bills were more than I paid for college and I needed the surgeries badly. So while friends have been able to start to buy houses, get married, or go on vacations to find themselves, all my money has gone into buying the privilege to live a pain-free life. And I definitely feel left behind and frustrated. I've switched sales jobs a few times since with disastrous results. I feel like I'm in a dead-end career without any hope of living without roommates ever. And I'm incredibly angry that to be able to advance into any other field I need a graduate degree which will only add to the debt I already have. It feels like there's no winning and nothing to look forward to other than working to pay off debt. At this point, I'm so burnt out on sales and so unhappy I'm applying to free CNA training programs because I'm desperate to feel like my work has meaning. I can make twice as much doing sales cold calls annoying people over the phone all day than I can taking care of the frail and elderly. Which to me shows how broken our society is. The labor we actually need is underpaid and bullshit is valued. I know my immigrant father will be disappointed in me doing the same work he does, but I give up. This is and has always been my place in society given my class, race, and social status. I'm tired of pretending it's not because I was given a fancy piece of paper no one gives a shit about. The only real long term goal I have anymore is to pay off enough debt to join a commune or buy a small piece of land to live off of. I don't think I'm depressed or unreasonably pessimistic about wanting to quit society especially with how COVID has revealed how our capitalist society is more than willing to slaughter thousands to prop up the stock market. If you aren't disgusted, you haven't been paying attention. I miss having hopes for the future yet hope seems naive. For now, all my happiness comes from tending to my garden with housemates, seeing my siblings and friends when I can, and the small hope that I'll be able to leave office work for good.

While I type this my new job is having me attend a zoom meeting with a top salesman spouting millionaire mentality/ positive thinking bullshit. This toxic positivity, as well as rise and grind culture, is so prevalent in our generation because admitting the truth that systemic change is needed is too hard for most of us to bear. I'd rather change adult diapers all day as a CNA than hear another lie about how a company cares about me or how anyone can be a millionaire. Success in this country is a birth lottery. And I can't express how freeing it feels to say that out loud.

As a society, we live in great stories and myths. This is particularly true for a society like the United States, where we do not have the myths and traditions of the old world to rely on. People came to the U.S. to escape all of that. However, we have created some of our own because humans need a story to tell themselves. Much of our pathos about the Constitution, the Founding Fathers, and American exceptionalism is all part of the great American myth. Few nations can claim an entire book has been written about them with a title like *Indispensable Nation* (Robert Lieber).

The great millennial myth came out of economic studies of the post-war period, and a new story was born: go to college, and you will be financially successful in life. The myth did not stop there either. The myth also included a few other items: do well in school and get good grades for a better college. Stay off drugs and stay out of prison so those won't be barriers to employment in the future. This modern narrative was borne out of the culture of the late 1970s and early 1980s right when Xennials and millennials were being born.

The college narrative began in earnest in the mid-1980s. The employment world was changing. Staying at a company for life was a thing of the past. Having the right skills and education to move forward in your career and to change jobs often was the new normal. Some commentators even went so far as to suggest that workers should look at themselves as a business of one.

The priority of the skills learned in education was a product of this change. Just as millennials were learning their ABCs and one, two, threes, their parents looked out at the changing job market and collectively, although unconsciously, decided that their children were going to face up to a better future and the best way to do that was through the personal investment of education. That is how education has been marketed; even now, it is an investment in oneself for better earnings and job opportunities.

Another aspect of this story was the long-term data showing that people with college educations made more money (up to $1 million, the oft-cited figure from the Department of Labor) over the life of their careers. Multiple government studies also found that college graduates were unemployed less often and for shorter periods. All the data about the boomers and Xers of the day pointed to the fact that college was the key to success in life. One aspect the data didn't consider was that most workers of the time didn't go to college and that those who did were often better educated to start with, coming from middle-class or better homes with the resources to prepare for college and be successful at college.

Millennials took this mythic message seriously. Buoyed by the booming economy of the 1990s, millennials made their first mistake. They tried to win the system. However, they were trying to win a system that actively ensured they would lose.

In *Not Working, Where Have All the Good Jobs Gone?* we see the economic structures that ensured millennials would remain poor. Firstly, young men have been left behind by the modern economy. Blanchflower says, "Many young men are falling to the bottom of the income ladder. In 1975, only 25% of men ages 25-34 had incomes of less than $30,000 per year. By 2016, that share had risen to 41% (using 2015 adjusted dollars)." He says, "Real weekly earnings for the United States for production and non-supervisory workers in 1982-1984 dollars have not recovered to 1972 levels. Weekly earnings are what matters, as this is about take-home pay. Real weekly earnings were $341.36 in 1972 compared with 311.80 in April 2018, down 9%."

The social consequences are dire, as seen in the NEETS chapter. Blanchflower is unequivocal when he says, "Long-term unemployment tends to cause significant mental and material stress for those affected and their families. It is also of concern for policymakers, as high long-term unemployment rates indicate that labor markets are operating inefficiently."

Leaving people out of the workforce and unable to exist like other adults costs society dearly. Blanchflower goes on to say, "Joblessness matters as it hurts. Long periods without work are harmful, especially for the young. For young people, joblessness can cause permanent scars and prevent family formation, including the need to have children and get married. Unemployment is stressful and hurts morale; it lowers self-esteem and increases susceptibility to malnutrition, illness, and mental stress. It raises the possibility of smoking, lowers life expectancy, and raises the possibility of suicide. The unemployed commit more crime."

It is not great for people or society when folks are out of work. However, wasn't college supposed to solve this problem? In the aftermath of the 2008 crisis, companies quit hiring many entry-level jobs, as we know. Instead of acknowledging this structural change in the economy, people just made fun of college grads working at Starbucks. There is a popular trope, especially in right-wing circles, about people who go to college to study incredibly useless subjects in the employment world. In most forums on Reddit over the past decade, the advice for getting a good job has been two-fold. The first piece of advice is to learn how to code, and the second is to go into the trades.

Although the idea that college should lead to ready employment, the laser focus of students on paying degrees is directly a result of the post-recession environment. Before 2008, when most millennials were going to college, a degree was a degree, and the subject you studied mattered far less. Companies often recruited people from major programs to train or work in certain areas of the company where they knew that people with a particular background would excel. Still others managed to parlay a degree in English literature into a variety of interesting roles where the link between education and job wasn't apparent but much more subtle.

In the post-recession environment, many millennials graduated with degrees, often in the humanities, and went looking for jobs only to find that there were none available for their degree program, or they were passed over for jobs because their degree did not match their nascent skills, or because they did not have a degree in an ever-narrowing list of specialty fields, usually in STEM. This is yet another extension of the millennial mantra: stay out of trouble, stay in school, and have a good life. These years would begin the end of many humanities programs at major universities. At a personal level, my two degrees in political science have become a running joke, a joke so bad that I have quit talking to people who make fun of the degree program. There was already an inside joke about how there has never been a job posting listed, "Political scientist wanted," but the fact that companies wanted ready-made workers without doing any training left many folks with humanities degrees, critical thinking skills, and the basis for a promising career out in the proverbial cold of the employment world.

Blanchflower also wrote, "A further factor (to why Americans feel worse about the economy) is likely that men's real earnings growth is well below that of women." This shift in economic dynamics has affected the dating market and family formation and has seen the rise of NEETs and incels (we will discuss involuntary celibates later). However, Blanchflower, in Chapter 1, got right to the point of why we have a structural economic issue that has disadvantaged millennials and now Gen Z. He wrote, "Millennials have been affected via inflation and deficit spending which drove up the cost of essentials like housing, healthcare, and food. The problem with the economy is demand." Another aspect he presented was: "Due to a lack of increases in wages (globalization, immigration, corporate manager salaries), wages have stagnated, and the prices of non-offshored goods and services have gone up due to inflation." And then he wrapped this up by writing, "There is a lack of goods demand and therefore labor demand because people do not have money to spend in part due to wages but also in part due to excess inflation."

CHAPTER 16:

YOUR BRAIN ON POVERTY

S ubmission from Reddit:

> I'm one of the "lucky" ones, maybe. 30M, to pay for university, I obtained my CPhT (certified pharmacy technician) and worked full time. Eventually the burnout killed me and I stopped attending, I still lived with my parents then. I met my now wife as she was starting out working. I was still in hospitals as a tech, it paid ok, but nothing spectacular, like 30k, she made similar, and with some help from my parents, we got a house as we married 5 years ago. A stint of unemployment nearly destroyed me, I was able to get a job at insurance making a little more, and each year I moved departments (surviving one layoff). We helped pay bills by having three housemates, now down to one. We have no kids, only recently have we been able to save money to really think about retirement. Many of my peers still struggle to be stable, many are stuck working minimum wage jobs even now, some haven't been employed at all in years.

We've managed to scrape some semblance of middle class, but it was so fucking tiring. I feel like I've lived a whole lifetime at 30. There was no room for error, I made the right choice numerous times and it was barely, through luck alone, enough. My fate was almost never in my hands, job loss now would still be almost unbearable. It's taken hundreds, maybe thousands, of applications, dozens of interviews to eke out a wage increase more than a pittance each year. Any lapse in vigilance would slowly lead to poverty. The world does not want us to succeed. All the while, someone with capital could have made as much as I have in a decade in a few weeks on the market. People owning yachts and shit because they come from money, while others less fortunate are homeless. We obtained the "American dream," and not only is it nothing special, the guilt of our relative success being a lottery sucks. I spend frivolously because the future is so uncertain, nihilism has been beaten into me. There is no bright eyed and bushy tailed in my world. We happened to avoid major catastrophes, that's it. If either of us had ever lost our ability to work, or needed major medical care, or any of our parents needed help, we'd not be where we are now, and others our age were not so fortunate.

If anything, I'm just happy I never became addicted to anything, God knows I don't disparage anyone who has given the environment.

In the United States, we have a somewhat paternalistic idea about poverty and poor people. We view it as a moral failing, not merely a cash problem. Any discussion of the systemic issues around poverty is quickly drowned out by people who admonish people experiencing poverty to simply work harder. Anyone who knows poor people knows that they work harder than their well-heeled peers. It is complicated to get a conversation going about how austerity policies, welfare-to-work, and trimming of benefits have left many people in a trap of poverty or, worse yet, living out of their cars while still working and unable to afford housing. This isn't even an American issue, either.

Blanchflower quotes the United Nations, "The United Nations Special Rapporteur on extreme poverty and human rights to the UK, Philip Alston, reported at the end of a twelve-day visit to the UK in 2018 that "the government's policies and drastic cuts to social support are entrenching high levels of poverty and inflicting unnecessary misery…in the fifth richest country in the world, this is not just a disgrace, but a social calamity and an economic disaster, all rolled into one." He continued: "Government policies have inflicted great misery unnecessarily, especially on the working poor, on single mothers struggling against mighty odds, on people with disabilities who are already marginalized, and on millions of children who are locked into a cycle of poverty from which many will have great difficult escaping."

The UK is a society with much more social support than the United States. The situation here in the United States is just as bad and, in many cases, far worse because of welfare reform, welfare-to-work programs, many states not choosing to extend Medicaid benefits through the Affordable Care Act, and a lack of public housing beyond Section 8 programs (the wait lists of which last years). At least people with low incomes in Britain can go to the hospital for free thanks to the National Health Service; in the U.S., they end up in debt.

Blanchflower says, "In the UK, the use of food banks is on the rise. In the United States, happiness is down for the least educated, and there is a deepening opioid crisis. There has been an increase in the United States in deaths of despair from drug and alcohol poisoning. This seems unlikely to be unrelated to the worsening economic position of many, especially white, non-Hispanic, middle-aged, working-class men and women with low levels of education."

Poverty is an insidious disease. Like any other disease, it affects the body and leaves scars that can last a lifetime. In a seminal article, "How Poverty Affects the Brain and Behavior," the Association for

Psychological Science summarized the situation: "Poverty lowers brain IQ and can cause people to make risky decisions."

The divide between those with resources and those without is stark. The article states, "The researchers found that rich participants tended to avoid high-cost borrowing, but poor participants were quick to take a loan, overborrowed, ran out of time faster, and ultimately left the lab with less money when the game was completed. Behavior like this often is attributed to people experiencing poverty being myopic and exhibiting less control, except that here, the 'poor' participants were Princeton students. Scarcity can affect even the privileged."

The study also found that poverty and mental illness are often linked. The study goes on to say: "Poverty affects mental health through an array of social and biological mechanisms acting at multiple levels, including individuals, families, local communities, and nations. Individual-level mediators in the relationship between poverty and mental health include financial stress, chronic and acute stressful life events exposure, hypothalamic-pituitary-adrenal (HPA) axis changes, other brain circuit changes (e.g., language processing, executive functioning), poor prenatal health and birth outcomes, inadequate nutrition, and toxin exposure (e.g., lead). Family-level mediators include parental relationship stress, parental psychopathology (especially depression), low parental warmth or investment, hostile and inconsistent parenting, low-stimulation home environments, and child abuse and neglect."

The idea of simply giving people cash or doing individual interventions is not enough to solve the problem, especially when systemic issues are at play. The Association for Psychological Science also wrote, "While assisting individual patients can have a significant impact, the repeated occurrence of poverty in the lives of our clients calls for community-level interventions. Addressing the social determinants of mental health through the healthcare system is only part of the answer, and creative solutions are needed. At the meso-level, which includes community engagement and education, training, and continuing professional development, mental health professionals can advocate for improved health. For example, they can develop outreach programs that target specific populations, they can contact local elected officials about the need for enhanced funding of social services, and they can provide continuing education sessions for their fellow health care professionals."

People in poverty have greater trouble with long-term thinking and many of the seemingly irrational decisions that poor people make begin to make sense. An article in the November 2013 issue of *The Atlantic* states: "In August, *Science* published a landmark study concluding that poverty, itself, hurts our ability to make decisions about school, finances, and life, imposing a mental burden similar to losing 13 IQ points."

This article was widely seen as a counter argument to claims that poor people are "to blame" for bad decisions and a rebuke to policies that withhold money from the poorest families unless they behave in a certain way. After all, if being poor leads to bad decision-making (as opposed to the other way around), giving cash should alleviate the cognitive burdens of poverty, all on its own."

Millennials have had much focus put on their spending habits. Advertising companies and businesses began studying consumer spending habits in the years after World War II, and the spending habits of baby boomers have been studied like a Bible for 40 years. They were ready for the spending habits of Gen X and millennials, and while Gen X was disruptive, it wasn't as disruptive as millennials would be. With funds short, napkins, laundry softeners, casual dining, and even diamonds have all been declared dead due to millennials not spending their scarce resources at TGI Fridays or on a laundry additive for softer clothing. Avocado toast has become a millennial trope as an example of our bad spending decisions. iPhones are a byword for wasteful things that young people should sacrifice to save money. Much like their Japanese peers, the reality for many millennials is that not having these items is a far greater cost than merely saving money that won't solve any currently pending problems. It would take a lot of avocado toast to afford a house.

POVERTY IN THE TWENTIETH CENTURY

We have a particular picture of poverty from the previous century. Poverty back then looked like missing indoor plumbing or lacking modern electric conveniences like a TV or a washing machine. Those living in the Depression would pack their meager possessions in a small cart or on the back of a Model A and try to improve their lives elsewhere. Film footage provided a picture of poverty that showed run-down tower blocks with rampant crime and peeling wallpaper. Poverty could mean too many children, living in the street, and having rags for clothes. This was the view common in popular culture as well.

In one scene from the famous prime-time soap Dynasty, Krystal Carrington (Linda Evans) has her purse stolen by a boy, and she chases him to a derelict dwelling behind a building where he lives with his family. They live in a shed in ragged clothes, which made for a stark picture against her modern-style fur coat, and blown-out hair.

In the years after World War II, slum clearance was essential to improving American cities and reducing poverty. The interstate highway system was used as an economic cudgel that broke apart communities and gave cities an excuse to tear down old, dilapidated housing and have the people who lived there move somewhere else.

Following that, President Johnson introduced the Great Society, which created several new programs, including food stamps Electronic Benefits Transfer / Supplemental Assistance Nutrition Program (EBT/SNAP), cash handouts, Temporary Relief for Needy Families (TANF), Medicare and Medicaid (healthcare), and Women, Children, and Infants (WIC), a special program for new mothers to help feed their children. Not since the New Deal had one administration pushed so hard to remake America in the image of a new sort of country where poverty was eliminated through government largesse. These programs sought to address public policy goals and scourges like malnourished children and elderly persons' healthcare needs. These programs have been largely successful despite being hampered by decades of compromise between the Republican Party, which would see them eliminated, and Democratic Party trying to save them at every turn. The War on Poverty was modestly successful. It wouldn't take long for conservatives to attack it, just as they had attacked the reforms of the New Deal. Reducing government spending on these programs empowered the Republican Party to enact bold legislation through the 1980s and 1990s to reduce the size and scope of the programs. Medicaid would not see expansion until the Children's Health Insurance Program (CHIP) and Affordable Care Act.

Given what we know about poverty in the 20th century, it is hard to say that anyone today is inferior. Back then, poor people didn't have cars and TVs. All but the homeless now have TVs (and some of the homeless even have cars!). It seems like smartphones are common as well. Despite all the numbers and effects of poverty, our collective image of poverty has never been updated to reflect the modern realities of poverty.

Modern poverty is often insecurity. It is being unable to handle an emergency expense. It is using payday loan services and not having stable housing. It means moving belongings in plastic bags from place to place. It means living in the same car that you drive to work. Poverty today might look luxurious as compared to the past, but it is no less psychologically damaging.

POVERTY BRAIN

The Association for Psychological Science (APS) published an article about some exciting experiments entitled "How Poverty Affects the Brain and Behavior."

"APS Fellow Eldar Shafir of Princeton University takes a different perspective on poverty, looking at its impact on behavior and decision-making. And the data shows that poor people make far more astute decisions than popularly believed; they weigh tradeoffs, pay special attention to prices, and juggle resources carefully," he said. However, their intense focus on stretching their scarce resources can absorb all their mental capacity, leaving them with little or no "cognitive bandwidth" to pursue job training, education, and other opportunities that could lead them out of poverty.

In a series of experiments, the results of which were published in 2013 in *Science*, Eldar Shafir, and his colleagues found that an individual preoccupied with money problems showed a decline in cognitive function akin to a 13-point drop in IQ (similar to losing an entire night's sleep).

The researchers began their study in a New Jersey mall, randomly recruiting 400 participants of various income levels. They asked subjects to ponder how they would solve hypothetical financial problems, such as paying for a car repair. Some participants were assigned an "easy" scenario, such as the mechanic's bill running just $150, while others were assigned a "hard" scenario, like the repair costing $1,500. The participants mulled over these scenarios as they performed some tests designed to measure fluid intelligence and cognition. Subjects were divided into "poor" and "rich" groups based on income.

The researchers found that both groups performed equally well on the tests in financially manageable scenarios. But when faced with complex scenarios, participants in the poor group performed significantly worse on the tests than those in the affluent group."

The psychological burden of not being able to reach the milestones of life is staggering. It isn't a wonder that people in the millennial generation are despairing at their circumstances in life. Having children has been delayed, as has buying a house. These problems are not just faced by the poorest. Even those with good salaries are struggling, as seen in some stories in this book. It is hard to feel like an adult when you look around at your life, and you can't seem to afford anything in your life that says, "Hey, I've made it." Americans eat avocado toast and lease another iPhone while the Japanese buy another Gucci bag, which is similar behavior. The psychological toll doesn't end there.

Millennials have been hard hit in their young lives. For those born between 1980 and 1997 (or 1999), the world has been full of tragedy, financial crosses, and a changing economy that has left many behind, no matter their background. Indeed, wealth has often been the only bulwark against the headwinds faced by the largest generation in U.S. history. However, those headwinds are also becoming deadly. It is important to remember that most people in this generation are from 25 to 45 years of age. The oldest millennials over 40 are sometimes called Xennials. This issue is not angsty teens with problems. The deaths of despair are happening to honest, adult people.

STRESSORS

Some of the increase of deaths among millennials is also because young adults are in more stressful environments, like the military and correctional facilities. Contrary to the idea that millennials are lazy, this generation has fought in America's long wars over the past twenty years. Many have returned either physically or emotionally disabled, with loss of their sanity and sense of normalcy. The school-to-prison pipeline has adversely impacted this generation. The advent of police officers at schools has turned routine behavioral offenses into criminal offenses. This has left young people trying to start life with a criminal record and trauma from the corrections system. All of these things, taken together, have left many millennials feeling hopeless, hapless, and helpless in the face of a system that seems to have been determined not to let them in.

ECONOMIC CHANGES

The Association for Psychological Science report said that the rise in young adults living at home is partially responsible for the growth in luxury goods sales. Radio personality Dave Ramsey weighed in with some thoughts about the trend. "Let me get this straight. You're living in your mama's basement, but you've got a Coach purse," he said. "This is not parenting. This is coddling." Much like their Japanese counterparts, young people, mainly Gen Z but a few millennials, are buying high-end consumer goods instead of trying to move out into a hostile real estate market or do anything else. The logic is simple: you can't afford an apartment or a house, but a Gucci bag is achievable.

The greater portion of this generation came of age and looked for their first jobs right when the financial crisis struck. This is combined with how the gig economy rose at the same time companies essentially eliminated any position that could be called entry-level and did not allow employees to train on the job. This was combined with the fact that many low-skill jobs have been eliminated or automated away. These trends have never reversed since the recession; if anything, they have only worsened.

This is the first generation to enter a truly globalized job market. Younger workers are competing with workers from all over the world simultaneously, and the economic horrors of globalization for developed countries have been laid bare. Millennials entered the job market with this already in place. Older workers suffered through offshoring and outsourcing, and that was devastating enough. Millennials always had to compete globally, and to some degree, the deck was already stacked.

Much of the focus on the job market has been on how it has affected older workers and how much they have been left out of the American economic recovery and economic story. But the reality is that at least they were a part of the story and are still a part of it. Many millennials never even got into the book to start with. They were simply left behind, and for those born between 1986 and 1991, their economic future will always remain poor. They will never recover the lost wages they didn't earn during those jobless days in 2008-2011. They will not get back the interest from savings or the return on retirement investment. They will earn less over their lifetimes, and their situation will most likely always be somewhat precarious.

SOCIAL CHANGES

Much of the social changes that are now common in the mainstream media have to do with cultural changes around race, gender, and gender relations. However, it is important to remember that while millennials often push for these changes, they are also affected by how different the world is from how it was before. Millennials, especially the younger cohort, have borne the brunt of the changes in campus sexual assault policies. The laws around domestic violence, child support, and other modifications made when they were children have adversely affected them as adults. It may seem like younger people are better able to handle social change, but that isn't always the case.

Dating has also changed, profoundly affecting this generation, especially young men. Online dating has broadened our ability to find a partner and a mate, creating a scenario where young people are not just competing with people in their town, city, or neighborhood. They are competing with people from anywhere with an internet connection. It is among this generation we've seen the rise of incels (the involuntarily celibate), men's rights activists (who have some legitimate gripes), and the recruitment of young white males to the far-right organizations like the Proud Boys. The culture of casual and readily available sex without much in the way of commitment has had effects that are not yet understood. Simon Sinek likes to blame it on a culture of instant gratification that gives us what we want when we want it. This is anti-thetical to dating in his mind. The picture isn't that simple. Competing with other men and women in your local area is one thing. Competing with strangers from miles away in an app is quite another.

This was the generation of men who failed to launch while the women crowded into schools to get degrees and were introduced into the lousy job market already mentioned. Men were written about in books and discussed in the media as feckless gamers without wanting to become "real men." Jordan Peterson has fixed that part of his entire business model. Women have not had an easier time. Not only do they have to handle all the stressors as mentioned above, but the world is often not friendly to women.

Starting families has been difficult as well. Families that do form struggle with childcare costs, and many millennials have opted out of parenthood. Social and economic stressors have made the dating landscape difficult and have led to challenges that previous generations didn't have to face.

WHAT TO DO?

Solutions to the deaths of despair are not obvious or easy; they are deeply individual. It is hard to write public policy for social problems. However, some basic economic investments could curb many issues. Changes like universal childcare could help families and encourage people to have children again. Creating a more equitable society will not give millennials back lost time. However, it can make a better future for everyone, and given this data, it might save lives.

CHAPTER 17:

ASSETS AND LABOR

A submission from Reddit:

Hard work pays off. Things will get better. To be successful, you need to go to college, and then you can be a productive member of society. I often heard these cliches from the adults around me growing up. During my time on this planet, I've experienced quite a lot and have seen so much change over the years. These tidbits of wisdom from my elders were anything but genuine and have me questioning many things about life.

I grew up in the Northeast and remember using a computer as a small child. My mother was forward-thinking, and our family's first computer was a Commodore 64. I remember my brother used to play computer games using a joystick! Over the years, we have gotten a new computer, and technology has rapidly changed: floppy disks, zip disks, and dial-up internet to DSL. Learning new information transitioned from World Book to Microsoft Encarta to Wikipedia. Things were changing so fast every few years.

My days of youth were full of sleepovers, playing freeze tag and kickball, and catching lightning bugs. But during my childhood years, tragic national events began to erode my childhood naivete. I remember in elementary school the Oklahoma City bombing, how all of the adults around me were in shock. We even had a discussion about it in class.

Then in middle school, Columbine happened. My older brother at that point was in high school. Slowly the innocence of American life was crumbling a little bit more. Bit by bit being able to move socially up in rank seemed to be getting more distant.

By the time I got to high school, I experienced what would be our generation's Kennedy assassination: 9/11. It was such a somber day. I remember being in, I believe it was history class, and there was an announcement over the PA. A bunch of us rushed to the cafeteria where there were TVs. We were watching the news and saw the second plane crash into the twin towers. It was so surreal. Seeing that second plane crash on TV, it looked like I was watching a blockbuster movie. Classmates had parents and relatives that commuted to the WTC. It was so wild. Our whole community mourned.

Life was different after that day. I did everything my parents wanted me to do, but would it be enough? My afternoons were filled with extra-curricular activities and I took honors classes. I distinctly remember my parents insisting that I go to college, and a four-year college at that. It wasn't even a request; it was a command. I even went to study abroad while still in high school hoping it would help me stand out from other college applicants.

My parents divorced when I was a teenager and during this time the court ruled that my father would pay for my college tuition. One thing that I really kick myself for is not going all in and making myself as competitive of a college candidate as possible. I trusted my father and thought he would pay for my college tuition. It wouldn't be too expensive for him, and he was court-ordered to do so. He was even making six figures and I had in-state tuition at my state's flagship university. The reality was by the time I would graduate with my degree I would also be saddled with thousands of dollars in student loans.

Trying to be more practical minded, I pursued my studies in business economics. I figured that I would be able to find a job in business and with economics being something I was interested in, it would be a breeze. Unfortunately, there was the 2008 Great Recession by the time I graduated. I was able to get a research assistant position at a top-notch university with a high-profile economics researcher, but then he went on leave and I had decided to matriculate into an economics post-graduate studies program.

During that time studying, I made poor decisions and had limited funds. I was studying abroad doing graduate studies in a rather expensive city. I was eating one or two meals a day at most because I couldn't afford anything more. Tired and downtrodden, I returned to the States without even earning my graduate certificate in Economics.

By this point, I was very depressed. While staying by my father's, I worked in retail at a store within walking distance and did some canvassing in a nearby city. Over time, I soon began feeling even more frustrated and depressed as I had no avenue out of my deadend job that I was working. My father then suggested that I work as a teacher; he himself worked in a school district as a social worker.

That's when I made the move to be close to my significant other and became a substitute teacher. At that time, it was difficult to get experience as a teacher. I worked for a few different districts and then I went on to being a teacher's aide. I figured if I worked as a teacher's aide, I could possibly snag a position as a teacher. Working in education taught me many things, being aware of workplace social landmines was one of them. Many of which I didn't navigate that well.

I put everything I had into becoming a teacher. After five years of being in the same district, I decided it was best for me to depart and look elsewhere as I was still a part-time teacher's aide. I take full responsibility for staying there for so long. It was not a good idea. I figured that I needed to work my way up in that school, but that was not happening.

During those five years, I worked with struggling readers, gained some teaching experience in rough inner-city schools. I was attempting to build my teaching resume, so I could hopefully have a chance to get a teaching position. I even worked multiple jobs in tutoring positions and went to night classes. All while also sending out resumes, attending job fairs, and networking. I even attended conferences to network with other teachers.

Other points in time were heartbreaking. I was offered a maternity leave position by a neighboring district but was declined by the superintendent not approving my hire even though the Principal and Assistant Principal of the school extended an offer. Reluctantly and with resignation, I decided to take a long-term substitute teaching position for the remainder of the school year.

While I was busy whittling away at attempting to achieve my goals, I noticed that every day when I showered after

I got out, I would break out in hives. I thought it was very strange and brushed it off as just some skin sensitivity I was having to the soap I was using. I went to an allergist, and I was always so sensitive. I found out what foods and other environmental allergens my body reacted to. I put that all in the back of my mind and continued to persevere in trying to obtain a teaching position.

Over the years, I tried to move out of the school I was working in but was blocked. Even went to job fairs applying to private schools as well, but to no avail. In the end, all the hard work paid off, I finally was able to get a permanent teaching position in an inner-city school district.

When I started working at the inner-city school, I moved back in with my father. Unfortunately, I had to pay rent. He did help me in some ways. He worked with a similar population and helped me navigate and formulate plans on how to best approach situations. The thing was, now that I look back, I believe I was in over my head. During that first year as a teacher, I was absolutely exhausted and stressed out. I developed a good rapport with my students, but found that other staff and administrators were not that supportive.

Strangely enough, I'd have these bouts where I felt so weak and tired I could barely move. My pulse rate would slow down as well. Because of these persistent symptoms, I decided to go to the nurse's office. The nurse asked me if I was anemic or had any thyroid issues. I told him I did not. Or at least none that I was aware of.

Upon hearing what he told me, I made sure to go to an annual checkup with my doctor and had hormone tests run. Nothing out of the ordinary. I figured I was feeling run down with the daily stress of worrying I could get shot or mugged leaving the school building to dealing with a high strung coworker. I was also averaging six hours of sleep at most each night. After that school year concluded, I got laid off because there was a cut in funding and decided to transfer to another school in the same district.

As it was like last year, I continued taking night classes to improve my craft in teaching. At this point I took on a different role where I had a lot more responsibility. The beginning of the school year was met with a new set of coworkers and a completely different set of workplace rules. I tried the best I could to keep up. To my dismay, I found that I was gradually getting more and more work thrown my way.

That's when the fatigue started to become a constant staple in my life. At this point, I was no longer living with my father. Instead I moved into a house with roommates because the salary I got as a teacher didn't afford me enough to get my own apartment in a safe area. And with my night classes, I had to ensure that I wasn't going to be assaulted walking through my neighborhood.

It was becoming clear that this persistent lethargy was not something I could shake off. Having a major sleep deficit while being crushed under the weight of my workload from my night classes and full-time duties did not help me in the matter. Things continued to get worse for me physically. I was still getting hives after showering and now I noticed my hair was falling out, even my scalp was scaly in appearance. At work, I had moments where my heart would race and would vacillate between fast and normal pace. Due to my exhaustion, I had to take naps every day during the workday. It got to a point where I had to take off once a week to just rest myself because I was feeling so exhausted.

And it continued to get worse. I'd arrive at work and before the first period would even start to feel as exhausted as if I had run a marathon or as if I had pulled an all-nighter. Strangely enough, I also had these episodes where my body became so weak I couldn't even pick up a pencil or book and I had to have my students help me by passing things out to the other students. During these episodes, I couldn't even walk across the room; I resorted to rolling myself slowly across the room in a computer chair. This was accompanied by dark circles around my eyes and becoming very pale.

My body was falling apart. My mental health was deteriorating. I found myself feeling not only depressed all of the time, which was out of the norm for me, but I also was becoming increasingly suicidal. Speaking to the head of the school, I had expressed my concerns several times, but it fell on deaf ears. And all I was expected to do was to push through. "You're young," he'd reassure me. "You're just tired because of all the things you are doing." Others reassured me in the same way. But I had a gut feeling that something was horribly wrong.

The final straw was when I was walking up the stairs to go back to my classroom and I collapsed on the stairwell. At that moment, I knew I had had enough.

I put in for a personal leave and got the paperwork completed that very same day. Being on leave, I was able to finally make appointments with doctors and not fear any interference with workplace protocol. First I went to the OBGYN to get my hormone levels tested. I suspected that the underlying cause to my unexplained fatigue was the culprit of imbalanced hormones.

I got the test results back and the nurse informed me of the anomaly in my thyroid hormone. She strongly suggested that I seek out an endocrinologist to get further testing. After researching different endocrinologists in the area, I selected one that accepted my insurance and made an appointment. It took some time to be able to see her, but when I finally did I was able to get some more answers.

She had me take another blood test. After explaining to her my workplace situation and my unexplainable episodes, we discussed it was highly probable that it was an autoimmune disease affecting my thyroid. The results would be in and I would see her the following week.

The following week it was confirmed by the blood tests that indeed I had the suspected thyroid disease. She even mentioned to me that she was glad that I came to see her when I did because if I didn't, I would have been in the hospital for weeks!

I also ended up going to a cardiologist and had to be on a heart monitor for two weeks. Come to find out after that that I also have a heart condition where my heart skips beats at times [it was] the solution to these ailments that plagued me. Well, there isn't a cure per se, but it would be best for me to manage my stress levels, get to a healthy weight (I was about 20 pounds underweight at the time), and work on taking things one day at a time.

After much deliberation, I decided that I would reunite with my then fiancé, now husband. I ended up resigning from my job to salvage my health as returning would just worsen my health condition all over again.

After all the things that people older than me told me, I've come to the conclusion that much of it was what worked for them. Many of them don't have answers that are workable solutions for our generation. A lot of success comes from luck, not just hard work and literally killing myself because others are judging my worth in society was not worth it in the end.

I guess I should try to end this on a happy note. Although my health condition has not gone into remission, I haven't had to have an increase in my medication. I moved to a state that is sunny most of the year and I am coming to terms with my mental and physical health aspects in my life. In the past few months, I did manage to get a few part-time jobs so I could gradually make my way back into the workforce. Unfortunately, the pandemic hit and those jobs got cancelled.

I'm learning to take things in stride and try the best that I can. I'm learning that when people say things it's not a fact for everyone. Maybe it worked for them, but I find that it is becoming increasingly more difficult for each succeeding generation. All I can do is strive for progress not perfection. Life is uncertain. Life is constantly changing. Most things are outside of our control.

Millennials were the first generation that had to compete in a global labor force and their labor was too expensive due to the high cost of living in the United States. U.S. workers are the most expensive in the world and the corporations who could offshore their operations to cheaper countries did so in a big way beginning right about the time millennials were looking to start their careers in the early aughts.

It is no secret that in our modern economy, the people who are making the money are those who already have money. Over the past decade since the great financial crisis, the Federal Reserve has dumped money into assets which has propped up the housing market and the stock market. From *The Theft of a Decade*, "One of the most disastrous decisions for millennials concerns monetary policy and the Federal Reserve. The special sauce America had been missing since the 1970s was a productive investment. Yet instead of trying new policies to finally lift investment out of its generation-long funk—let alone its Great Recession stagnation—the Fed tripled down on the monetary policies that had distorted investment for decades already."

The Great Recession is something I have spent time studying. I've watched *The Big Short*, *The Flaw*, and other documentaries on the financial crisis. I've read *Too Big to Fail* by Aaron Ross Sorkin and watched the matching movie starring Cynthia Nixon from *Sex and the City*. I wrote a play for a 24-hour theater festival, and I imagine a world where Hank Paulson gives a full-on interview in the middle of the crisis and answers all the questions people would have liked him to talk about in the middle of the crisis. I've read as much as I could find on the Great Recession, and I even tried to contact Dick Fuld at one point. I just wanted him to answer one question, "Why did you do this to us? Why did you destroy our lives?"

The Great Recession is one of those life events that changed everything. For many Americans, this was a double blow. Just seven years before, we had been attacked by a foreign power on our own soil, something that hadn't happened in the contiguous United States since the war of 1812, as traumatic as Pearl Harbor before it. The magical world of the 1990s and Pax Americana was immediately broken as the World Trade Center was destroyed on an otherwise pleasant Tuesday morning in September.

Seven years later, when the Great Recession began, the world changed again. In the intervening time, America had gone to war in Afghanistan. While victory had been declared early on when the Taliban government had been toppled, and the charismatic Hamid Karzai was installed via popular election, the war was not going well. The war in Iraq wasn't going any better. The 2003 invasion had seen a rapid takeover of the country despite the horrors of the battle of

Fallujah. Protests on the justification for that war had begun in 2005, shortly after the re-election of George W. Bush in 2004. The country had learned more about weapons of mass destruction than most people had ever wanted to know about them, and it had become evident that not everything about the war in Iraq was as it seemed. The years following would see the U.S. directly occupy Iraq through the occupational authority and then see a peaceful transition of power to a popularly elected Iraqi government. The weapons of mass destruction (WMDs) were never found, and the Iraq war is often seen as one of the most unjust wars the United States has engaged with to date. Both of these wars went on longer than Vietnam, although with smaller but still significant body counts.

The year 2008 was a presidential election. Senator John McCain of Arizona, himself a critic of the Iraq war and a prisoner-of-war Vietnam veteran, was running against a young Senator from Illinois named Barack Hussein Obama, who, thanks to his Kenyan father, was running to be America's first black president. The early cracks in the housing crisis had begun in the fall of 2007. By the summer of 2008, the crisis was in full swing, with major investment banks like Bear Sterns, Merrill Lynch, and Lehman Brothers teetering on the brink of collapse. Bigger banks like Bank of America and Goldman Sachs had better balance sheets, but questions were already rising. At Citibank, a new CEO, Vikram Shankar Pandit, was supposed to calm investors, but that move already showed its limitations.

Alongside this crisis, the big federal housing lenders Fannie Mae and Freddie Mac had been nationalized to save them and prevent the totality of their debt and defaulting mortgages from falling back on the taxpayer. This would represent just the beginning of the crisis. When Hank Paulson attended the Beijing Olympics, even the Chinese, large holders of U.S. debt and investors in Fannie and Freddie, expressed a quiet East Asian concern about what was happening with the mortgage lender. Another industry that would soon be exposed to public view is home mortgages.

The COVID-19 pandemic only made this worse. Government policy has prioritized assets over wages and shifted that decision's fiscal burden onto millennials. In *The Theft of a Decade*, we read, "Mulligan argues that these labor-market distortions slowed the recovery, a phenomenon he calls the redistribution recession. The implications for millennials are serious. All this additional stimulus spending was funded by debt, especially on the transfer payments to help households. As a result, the net effect was to shift some of the economic burden of the Great Recession from the current generation onto future generations of taxpayers... That leads to a troubling conclusion: the greatest fiscal theft of all that boomers have perpetuated over the past decade is to rob their millennial children of fiscal choice. Millennials increasingly find ourselves left with no good options for fixing all these problems."

For millennials, the setbacks of the Great Financial Crisis and the pandemic have made their personal financial lives nearly untenable. The pandemic erased the housing gains made by millennials although some did purchase with the low interest rates offered at the time. Others were still unable to buy a house. News stories about Gen Z moving back in with parents was accompanied by younger and even 30-something millennials marching back to their parents' homes as well.

THE NEW ECONOMY

Knowledge work does not employ masses of people, and knowledge work does not trickle down to the greater economy like a factory job. It's a matter of scale. The old canard of this phenomenon is Instagram. When Instagram was purchased by Facebook (now Meta), it only had fourteen employees and was one of the biggest apps in the world. The new economy can do tremendous things but employs far fewer workers than the industrial economy. Industrialization worked because a large amount of labor was needed to work on the new machines and at the new assembly lines. The new economy is dominated by people on laptops who can have a great effect without nearly as much human effort. When people think of the effects of automation, they usually think of factory workers displaced by large robots, but computers have had their effects, too.

Malls and other retail outlets are going under because the class of people with money to spend but aren't rich is too small to support retail as we know it. Luxury brands are doing well. Dollar General is doing well. JC Penney is going under.

CHAPTER 18:

MILLENNIALS AND POLITICS

A submission from Reddit,

I'm not really sure how to begin and I have a tendency to get sidetracked when I tell stories, but I'll try. I'm 28, turning 29 this year (2020), Caucasian Male.

I don't come from money. Up until I was eight, we lived in a trailer park, but around that time we moved to a much larger, nicer trailer park. We had a double wide, an acre of land, and we never went hungry, but I definitely wouldn't call it easy living. There wasn't a lot of room in the family budget for frivolous spending. We were still using a Gateway 98 PC in 2006, and Dad supplemented our food budget by hunting deer every year. Things were hard, but never this hard. We always found ways to have fun, to go out and do stuff, traveled around our State and its nearest neighbors. I know there are tons of people who had it worse than I did growing up.

All my problems started when I was maybe 13 or 14. See, I loved learning. As much as I actually hated going to school,

I wanted an education. I wanted to be a professional, to have a good job and a good future. My mom dropped out of college and didn't go back until she lost her job prior to the recession. My whole life, she drilled into my head how important college was: A college education was the end-all-be-all as far as she was concerned. She didn't care what school I went to so long as I went for at least a Bachelor's degree. She really didn't even care what I wanted to go to school for, as if she thought that a college degree was some kind of Golden Ticket that automatically led to a better, more prosperous life. Looking back on it now, I understand she was trying to live vicariously through me. She was ashamed that she had given up on her college dream, ashamed at her mediocre academic career, and I think that her reaction to that shame and her own failures was to see me as some kind of redemption play. It was almost like she thought that if I succeeded where she failed, it would somehow magically erase her own fuck ups. Either that, or she was grooming me to be her personal parachute: an 'Escape Hatch,' since with all the debt she'd wracked up there was absolutely zero chance she'd ever have a proper retirement.

Problem was, I was a curious kid. When no one could give me an answer that satisfied me, I did my best to find the information on my own. This was the Dawning of the Internet Age, so naturally I spent a lot of time on message boards and chat rooms, and eventually here at Reddit on an account I've since retired. At fourteen, I was being exposed to all kinds of information, and I really didn't know how to process it all. A lot of Middle and High School was spent researching college and prospective career paths, and while I found more than a few that seemed like good fits for me, I was always horrified by the amount of money I'd end up spending.

As '08 loomed closer and closer, I was becoming increasingly aware of just how much a college degree would cost, and since my parents argued about money and debt on a weekly (if not nightly) basis, I was painfully conscious of the fact that the only way I'd ever pay for a college education was with loans and scholarships. As the Recession came into its full swing, my parents' relationship continued to deteriorate. With one exception, my grades were going strong, but as things at home got worse and worse, my grades started slipping, and my mom started becoming almost desperate to shove me off to college ASAP. She was emotionally and psychologically abusive, not to an extreme, but enough that it left a mark. To this day, I still don't know if she's even capable of recognizing the role she played in everything that came next.

The more pressure she put on me, the more I failed to meet her expectations of scholarly perfection, the more hits my self-esteem took. Somehow, my already angsty and depressed teenaged brain took her treatment of me as an assessment of my worth. If I couldn't even meet my own mother's standards, how could I ever earn a scholarship, even a little one, when I was competing with people who were so much more deserving of it than a failure like me? The more my parents fought about money, the more we had to tighten our belts and all that crap, the more afraid of debt I became. In the end, when I graduated high school, I didn't even want to go to college.

Don't misunderstand me: I wanted to pursue a higher education. I had seen what working in a factory for his whole life had done to my father, how little he had reaped from his labor. I did not want that to be my life. I wanted to make a difference, a REAL difference. I wanted my work to matter, not just to me, but to the people around me as well. I wanted to use my brain to make the world, in some way, better. I just didn't want to swallow a 100k debt to do it.

I tried so many times to explain the way I felt about College to my mom, but she never listened. All of my concerns were brushed aside, as if they didn't matter. I can't even remember how many times I was told I was just being too negative or pessimistic, and I'm self-aware enough to admit that there was some truth to the accusations, but I had legitimate fears and concerns. Instead of helping me work through them, my mom just kept shoving me towards college.

Like the weak, cowardly child I was, I folded. I picked a school, picked a course, and moved to the other side of the continent. My mom was so proud I was finally off to college, but really? I picked the school farthest away from home just to get away from her.

At first, I tried not to think about the debt I was wracking up as weeks turned into months. I couldn't keep up with the course work though. I'd picked Computer Science, but because I was an ignorant moron, I had no idea how much I didn't know about programming. I'd never written a line of code in my life, but this school swore up and down it could compress a 4-year degree into two and that you didn't need prior experience to make it work. I tried to roll with it, but as my grades kept dropping lower and lower, it became all too apparent that I was incurring debt for nothing. I dropped out after my first semester, moved back home. The pressure to get back into school, to pick a new college and a new course and try again? That started before I'd even gotten back home.

I was just...so angry at the time. I'd been so convinced that lying sack of shit Obama was going to fix all of this. I'd bought his 'Hope and Change' spiel hook, line, and sinker. I can't even begin to describe how much it hurt to realize the person I'd put so much faith in was nothing more than a two faced hypocrite. I'd convinced myself that if I just waited a little longer, the Occupy Wall Street Movement would break some ground, force a change. I was certain that any day, we'd find out that college was now free of charge and we could all pursue our dreams, build a better society than what we grew up in.

I even caved in and went back to school at a state university when my mom's passive aggressive needling and badgering became too unbearable. Surely, I thought, even if Tuition Reform still meant paying what I owed up to a certain point, that was better than not having a degree. Time dragged on, though, and living in the same house as my mom again left my mental health in shambles. I dropped out again, convinced that the degree I was pursuing would never get me a job that would pay down my debt. By then, my parents had finally divorced. I didn't have any money, and there weren't many career opportunities in the area I'd grown up in, so I moved to a local city with my mom and younger brother. Eventually she decided she was gay and married a woman I'm not entirely sure didn't molest her as a child. She moved to Florida, and my brother and I were left pretty much on our own. Dad was still around at the time, but mom had fucked him so thoroughly in divorce court that he wasn't in a position to help us. She'd even managed to cheat my brother out of a good chunk of the child support she'd fought tooth and nail to get from our dad.

I was pretty well broken by then. I smoked loads of weed, drank alcohol on an increasingly frequent basis. I tried to go to community college, but they needed tax information from my parents since I was under 24. Dad came through with his, mom didn't. So I figured I'd wait a few years and get in on my own.

As those years dragged on, however, things just kept getting worse. I had to work my ass off just to scrape by, and as more and more people began speaking out about how thoroughly screwed they were with the debt that came attached to their increasingly worthless degrees...I gave up on college.

I kept assuring my family I'd get back into school someday, but deep down, I was terrified of that debt. I kept working shitty jobs, I kept grinding on, and kept falling apart.

Now I'm here. Almost thirty, a High School degree that (up until this whole COVID-19 shitshow) had about as much value as toilet paper, and absolutely no hope for the future. I work in a factory now, just like my dad. I think I might even be making more than he did. He's so proud of me.

At first, it really wasn't all that bad. I kept up a winning attitude, I made all the right sounds and facial expressions to assure my family that I was 'happy' with my lot in life, but really, deep down? I was miserable. Things only got worse when I was moved to a different part of the plant. The work was much harder, the conditions harsher, the hours were longer. My manager was (and still very much is) a complete and utter piece of shit boomer I wouldn't piss on if he were on fire. He absolutely delights in punishing 'snowflakes' for having the audacity to even exist. I've been at this job for almost four years now.

This is the hard part. I wanna preface it by stating I understand full good and well that I am much better off than many, many people. Believe me, I understand, I have no right to bitch or complain, and if I had any self-respect I'd keep my mouth shut and be grateful to even have a job, but I just can't. I'm gonna try my best to sort out my thoughts and feelings, but please understand it's probably gonna be dark.

I don't want to be alive anymore. I haven't wanted to be alive for years now. Every day, I wake up, and I wish I had died in my sleep. I'm not suicidal: I cannot be clear enough about this, I have absolutely zero desire to kill myself. I'm not an immediate danger to myself or anyone else. I've been dealing with these feelings long enough that I can keep the worst of it in check, but I'm not oblivious to their presence. My job isn't particularly difficult, though I'm fit enough that I probably just haven't hit the physical wall yet. Mentally though, it grinds me down to nothing in about an hour. I perform the same series of very simple, very basic tasks over and over and over again for eight to ten hours a day, five to six days a week. I'm hot, I'm sweaty, I'm usually a little sore, but all of that is nothing compared to the war being waged in my head.

I don't smile. I don't really talk all that much to my coworkers. I've got nothing to share with more than two or three of them. Even if I had something to say, it's almost impossible to hold a conversation in the plant with all the fucking noise. So I do my job, I keep quiet. My head is just filled with an endless soliloquy of all my faults and failures. My insecurities and anxieties run riot over my gray matter. When I'm not at work, it's easy to shove them aside. It's easy to distract myself with a book or a show, or a game, or some little writing project that popped into my head. Well, it used to be easy. With each passing month it got harder and harder for me to do, well, anything. I used to love to cook, but now I barely have the time for it. I read the entire series of *A Song of Ice and Fire* in about two weeks? I've been working on *The Ultimate Hitchhiker's Guide to the Galaxy* for about a year now.

I used to write like fucking Hamilton, but now I can only do it when I've had a few days off from work and a bowl or two of weed. Otherwise I just stare at a blank page until I lose any and all motivation. Even when I do manage to knuckle down and start writing, I never finish anything.

"I don't have any hope left in me. I'll never further my education. I know that now. It's too damn late, and even if it wasn't? I can't fit college into this schedule. I can't afford College. If I quit my job to pursue an education, I'd be homeless and dead before the end of the year. I'm stuck in a job I hate, doing work that doesn't satisfy me or fulfill me in any way. Worse than that, the work I do? Building cars? It kills me. I believe in Climate Change, Ok? There's no pleasure in building cars when I know damn good and well every car that rolls off the production line is another nail in Planet Earth's coffin.

I can afford to keep myself well fed, housed, even somewhat entertained, but I could never afford a family. I've been paddling like crazy just to keep my head above water, but at the cost of my mental health. I'm such a fucking wreck of a human being, I could never even dream of inviting another person into my life. Why would I ever want to inflict that on another person? I'll never retire. I will never leave the U.S., never see the world, never have an adventure of any kind. My life is an endless cycle of waking up, going to work, and going to bed. I wake up wishing I was dead and go to bed despairing at my future.

All the while I keep tearing myself up inside. I'm so angry, so fucking tired, so god damn done that if someone told me to beg for my life, I'd tell them to put me out of my god damned misery. Why am I doing this? What's the point of putting myself through all this pain and misery? I chase a paycheck so I can live, but the price of earning that paycheck makes life unbearable. I used to have friends, I used to do things I loved, I used to feel like a human being.

Now I just feel like a robot made of meat.

Now I just want to cease.

God help me, I'm so fucking tired.

Often called the electoral dog who hasn't barked, as America's largest generation, millennials could really dictate American policy. Millennials and Gen Z combined dominated the 2022 mid-term elections. We've already seen a millennial run for President (Pete Buttigieg) and we millennials are in nearly every level of government. Although it was rather quixotic that Pete Buttigieg ran for President, despite only being the mayor of the third-largest city in Indiana, he gave us a preview of what a millennials president will look, sound, and feel like. However, for being such a large group of voters, millennials certainly are not in control of the political narratives in this country. Gen X isn't really in control of the narrative. Boomers in their 80s like Diane Feinstein (who died in office in September 2023) and Nancy Pelosi are just starting to retire, leaving room for younger people to step in and step up. So where is the millennial voice? In 1980, the boomers swept Ronald Reagan into power to express their own view of how America had changed, and they radically changed the country over the following eight years and followed it up with a vote for George H. W. Bush in 1988. The first baby boomer President, Bill Clinton, declared that the era of big government was over. Can millennials say that we have truly had our electoral say in the same way?

When the boomers decided to go to the polls in large numbers, Reagan became so popular that by 1984, he won forty-nine states, blowing Walter Mondale out of the water. If millennials wanted to flex their political muscle, they could seize government. But as Sternberg points out, millennials are still awhile away from truly taking over the major political parties much less the government. Again, boomers are helpful here. Boomers flexed their political muscle in the 1980s but the first Boomer president, Bill Clinton, wasn't elected until 1992. The oldest boomers were already 47 by that time. Even late cohort boomers (like my mom) were in their late 30s. For millennials, this means that we likely won't hit our political stride until the late 2020s and early 2030s.

It is often a mystery as to why more millennials don't vote. According to Sternberg in *The Theft of a Decade*, "Oh, and we vote or at least we can if we want to. The first election for the oldest of us was in 2000, and if the birth range for a millennial is 1982-1997, then all of the members of America's largest generation have been in the electorate since 2020. To date, millennials are the electoral dog that is choosing not to bark—younger turnout has always been low and there are signs that millennials vote in lower numbers than boomers did when they were our age." And the fact is that if millennials did bark, the bark would be quite loud as by 2024 millennials will be America's largest voting bloc.

TWO ERAS OF PROGRESS

Millennials want to believe in government. It is in our collaborative nature that has strong desires to work together as a group to achieve a certain goal. However, other generations on either side of millennials are far more suspicious of government. This has to do with the narratives around government. For boomers, the draft, Watergate, and Kent State reinforced anti-government narratives. For Gen X, the HIV/AIDS crisis and the Iran-Contra Affair further reinforced this narrative. For millennials it should have been the lies around the Iraq war, but many millennials were still in high school, and 9/11 came too soon as well. The 2008 financial crisis was blamed on the banks, not the government, and so the pandemic was really the first opportunity for millennials to get a taste of government not working well.

Policy wonk Nate Silver draws an interesting connection between this phenomenon and changing public attitudes toward the government over the latter part of the twentieth century: Nate Silver stated in *The New York Times*, "We may have gone from conceiving of government as an entity that builds roads, dams, and airports provides shared services like schooling, policing and national parks, and wages wars, into the world's largest insurance broker. Most of us don't much care for our insurance broker."

However, the problem with people, government, and millennials especially begins among their grandparents and the reforms of the New Deal. Sternberg writes of the New Deal reforms, "With the creation of Social Security and unemployment assistance programs in the 1930s, the government offered a financial backstop for those who lost their jobs, or for the elderly who hadn't been able to save adequately for their retirements."

The reforms of the New Deal were followed by sizeable social spending and change domestically in the years after World War II. The Bretton Woods economic system gave the U.S. a financial advantage to pay for all these new programs, fight the cold war, and send a man to the moon. This would come crashing down in 1971. Sternberg writes, "One reality was that to foster security and economic growth, the United States as a new superpower would have little choice but to play a much greater military role in the world. The Boomer's parents and grandparents made a serious fiscal mistake in the 1950s and 60s when they acted as if the higher level of U.S. military spending during the Cold War was only temporary. That might have seemed true initially when some analysts expected the Society Union and the Mao's People's Republic of China would collapse relatively quickly. But at a certain point, Washington should have realized that elevated military spending—which was almost nine percent of GDP in the 1960s and more than five percent of GDP on average through the 1970s and 1980s—was no longer what Alexander Hamilton would have considered an 'emergency.' It was a new and ongoing fact of life, and other parts of the budget should have adjusted in response."

But other parts of the budget didn't adjust. Our combined spending on the Cold War, Vietnam, the Apollo program, the war on drugs, and the Great Society reforms led to a collapse of the Bretton Woods systems and American prosperity in 1971 when Nixon took the U.S. dollar off the gold standard and let the currency free float. This set off a decade of trouble that included the oil crisis with the Middle East and outrageous interest rates and stagflation that would punctuate the malaise of the late 1970s. If the Kennedy, Johnson, and Nixon administrations had budgeted differently, they could have at least saved the Bretton Woods system. It is not that we couldn't have done all of those things, but we might have needed to reduce costs, especially in Vietnam. Some parts of the Great Society could have cost less. While glamorous, spending around the space program because Kennedy promised that America would put a man on the moon by 1969 also ran up government expenditure. His assassination made it seem like that promise had to be fulfilled in his memory and so the government put ten percent of GDP into the space program. The promise was fulfilled and the Cold War gambit proved American supremacy in space.

These two eras of progress would set up difficult economic times ahead. Layoffs began in earnest; entire companies and industries began to dry up overnight. Family farms collapsed too. Anyone depending on credit for business operations was crushed by eleven to seventeen percent interest rates. American business, which had operated smoothly for nearly thirty years, was grinding to a halt. The halt was not just caused by a change in economics or the collapse of the gold standard. Foreign competition had come into play. By this time, the economies of Japan and Europe had been rebuilt, and their goods were flooding onto American shores. Their technology was newer, faster, and more efficient. American industry hadn't competed internationally before, and its first outing was a rout.

Coming out of the 1970s, Paul Volcker would break the terrible inflation of the late 1970s. The petrodollar would help absorb most of the currency inflation. Reagan would be swept into office, promising to undo the regulatory environment that had seemingly caused the last decade of economic issues. Reagan was not a vanguard; he was a product of political and economic attitudes that had begun in 1951 with the Federalist Society, the John Birch Society, The Austrian and the Chicago Schools of Economics. Neoliberal economics (low taxes, low regulation, few social programs) had arrived, and it was here to stay.

Several U.S. presidents would assiduously tear apart the progress made between 1933 and 1971. Everything from trucking to airlines would be deregulated, taxes would be lowered, higher education would be defunded, mental healthcare would be defunded, welfare would be reformed, and people would be set free to "do what you do best," as Reagan would put it. These ideas had great appeal because people rightly believed they could do better independently without all the government interference that had become commonplace in the American economy over the twentieth century. What boomer voters in 1980 did not realize was that they were selling out the futures of their children and their grandchildren for temporary gains and the scion of "shareholder value."

Thanks to corporate capture of government, neoliberal economics have ruled the U.S. economy for millennials' entire lives. People still believe that if the wealthy and corporations don't get what they want, the terrible conditions of the 1970s will return. Since 1977, wealth has flowed away from productivity and workers and to the wealthy. Financialization and securitization in the 1980s and 1990s would accelerate this trend even further as the banking sector began to dominate more and more of the American economy. Goods were cheaper thanks to cheap overseas labor, but services skyrocketed in cost. In economic circles on social media, a familiar graph will be posted showing how the price of goods has fallen, and nearly everything has increased in price.

The boomers did well under this system. It's hard to deny it. Many have become wealthy in relative terms. Home ownership rates remain high among this generation. Retirement accounts are filled with trillions of dollars that bump around the stock market. Many boomers who came from modest backgrounds could be upwardly mobile in ways that seem to express the highest aspirations of the American dream. An economic boom did occur from 1993 to 2004. Alan Greenspan graced the covers of *Time* magazine and was proclaimed the master of the economic universe who had finally figured out how to manage the American economy.

However, this came at a terrible cost. Politics ground to a halt in functional terms because both major parties serve the corporate interest. As of 2024, the national debt, as a percentage of GDP, was at 124 percent, thanks to years of tax cuts extending back to Reagan. Wealth inequality has reached Gilded Age levels according to every measure, and the problem has become so severe that even the well-heeled folks at Davos and the World Economic Forum have realized that it has become a problem.

Politically, the boomers have controlled American politics since 1980. Their preferences, values, and desires have held the country hostage. Their seeming hostility to social programs of any kind, taxes, and their willingness to keep asset prices rising has prevented any mitigation of the worst effects of neoliberalism and austerity. Millennials and Gen Z look to Europe's generous social programs with envy of what this country could have had, and they wonder why we don't have those sorts of programs here. The answer is simple: their parents and grandparents voted to make sure those would never happen in this country. The small social safety net available has been pared back to be nearly useless.

Bernie Sanders didn't say anything new in his presidential runs of 2016 and 2020. Still, the reality is that he has a certain appeal to people who are suffering under a system that advantages the wealthy over everyone else. Young people, desperate for relief from the neoliberal system that put money in their parents' pockets at the expense of their security, flocked to Sanders. Unfortunately Sanders struggled to gain any real headway in achieving the democratic nomination, first against Hillary Clinton and then again against Joe Biden. His activism and popularity during the Occupy movement drove his campaign forward, but his policies didn't resonate with anyone over 40. Sanders attempted to break us out of the neoliberal trap that America has been living in, as created for us by folks like the Koch brothers (only one of whom is still living), and that has captured both major political parties. Younger people are ready for a different country, but that country is having difficulty being born.

MILLENNIAL ANTIPATHY

Millennials have often been called the electoral dog that has yet to bark. Millennials, as a group, are the most numerous generation right now. However, to look at America's politics, you wouldn't know it. The old divisions still form battle lines even though millennials are slowly gaining power at the national level on both sides of the aisle.

As a group, millennials are bucking a trend where people tend to get conservative as they get older. That isn't happening for millennials. Pollsters like Nate Silver and Steve Kornacki have remarked on this, which is not to say there aren't conservative millennials—they exist. However, the millennial generation, even its conservative parts, tends to be more liberal than their parents or grandparents. Even on popular culture war topics like LGBTQIA+ and abortion, younger people tend to be more open to progressive ideas on the issues. Even something as charged as gun control is popular among those under 45 in a bipartisan fashion.

Given this general feeling based on a variety of polls, even Fox News polls (especially around gun control) around these issues show that those under 50 are more open to change, and they often don't hold the same political charge. This can also be observed in the attitudes of the younger legislators at the national level. People like Matt Gaetz and Alexandra Ocasio-Cortez don't sound like boomer politicians, and both are known for different political views than Nancy Pelosi, Chuck Schumer, Tom Cotton, Mitch McConnell, or Lindsay Graham.

Trying to cause change is a lot of work. After Occupy fell apart, solving America's political issues seemed more difficult than anyone imagined. The boomers are not giving up power easily. The average age of members of Congress is 59. Millennials are in middle age and are only slowly beginning the process of taking control and trying to shift the system. Many have already abandoned change because of how many millennials don't vote. A Gen X friend recently told me, "I don't know why you millennials think you can change anything. We already went up against the boomers and lost. So now we're just starting businesses and making money off of crypto."

It's not exactly the encouragement that will inspire anyone to act. Forcing societal change is challenging, with so much of ordinary life precarious. Between student loans, housing issues, and low-paying jobs, who has time for governing? It seems this was designed for some people, but the reality is far more insidious. For many folks, it has always been this way. It was not until well into the 20th century that the working class enjoyed the labor protections that have become standard. Calls for an eight-hour workday, unemployment insurance, and other protections weren't enacted until the mid-1930s after nearly forty years of organizing on the part of labor.

For millennials, politics has always been complex. The intransigence of the Republican Party, while predictable due to the Tea Party, has been especially demoralizing. The year 2008 was the first election in which the bulk of the millennial generation could vote (the first presidential election in which we had millennial voters would have been in 2000). Obama was swept into power by the power of millennials. Obama promised Hope and Change, but there would be very little hope and change due to the rise of the Tea Party and six years of a Republican Party commitment to making sure that Obama accomplished little during his residency in the White House. This wasn't entirely unfamiliar for older millennials who had been voting adults in the 2000 election. Given how the GOP pulled strings in Florida and had the advantage of a conservative court to tilt things in the right direction to deliver George W. Bush to Washington, the Tea Party was more of the same old tricks. The decision of Bush v. Gore would change the course of the United States in the twenty-first century. Much of the popularity of Barack Obama was due to the unpopularity of George W. Bush and his forever wars in Iraq and Afghanistan, as well as the lies that surrounded those decisions. It would have always been a tall order for John McCain to overcome the Bush baggage.

The swirl of things that has happened politically in millennials' lifetimes has led to political antipathy. Gen X wasn't a generation to vote or be engaged (the slacker generation doesn't do voting), but millennials were missing from the 2010 midterms and only had a slight uptick in 2012. Things were better in 2016, but it was insufficient to tilt the election away from Donald Trump. The 2018 election showed a great deal of improvement, and the 2020 election turned out the way it did, in no small part, to millennials on both sides of the aisle. However, what isn't happening yet is the country prioritizing millennial policy issues and goals. President Biden has paid much lip service to issues like climate change, student loan forgiveness, and the lackluster job market. Still, little has been done to tackle the cost-of-living crisis or discuss issues severely affecting millennials. Our political dialogue still treats millennials as children who need their parents to fix their lives. Millennials are a diverse generation, and while it seems like everyone votes Democrat, that is far from true. One need only look at the people at a Trump rally to realize that the under-40 crowd is well represented. The arrests of men in various militias around the country in 2021 and 2022 show that millennials are as politically diverse as any other group. Is it a wonder that some millennials feel politically disengaged?

OCCUPY WALL STREET AND BOOMER POLITICS

Ronald Reagan led a relatively unsuccessful film career before he won the governor's mansion in California and, ultimately, the White House. Because Hollywood wasn't casting him, he got a job hosting the *General Electric Theater*. He started this job in the early 1960s. It seems odd now, but it was a trend at the time for major companies to advertise by sponsoring a whole hour of television. In the 1960s, GE was one of America's biggest companies and an eponymous brand—nearly every household had GE light bulbs or electric appliances. These shows often feature live performances, movies, or a variety of content. As part of his job as host and the face of the *General Electric Theater*, Reagan toured various GE facilities throughout the country.

Politics came up often in these conversations, and the theme was quite clear, as he would later state in his first run for governor of California. Middle-class, white-collar workers felt the New Deal economy was holding them back. They felt the regulations, price controls, and high worker pay slowly made American companies non-competitive with their rising foreign rivals. These workers were young, aspirational, looking for a chance to advance their interests. Early cohort boomers and silents were the primary people Reagan interacted with at these events.

The breakdown of the American economy was not just the breakdown of unions or wage stagnation—it was a concerted effort to take advantage of the interests of management over workers. As Jack Welch would demonstrate, he saved a failing and nearly bankrupt GE in the early 1980s, and the interests of management should align with the interests of shareholders. Rather than focusing on workers or customers, everything should be done at a company to produce shareholder value and express the will of the shareholders. In 2009, Jack Welch ended up criticizing that strategy. During his tenure, he cut 170,000 jobs from GE. However, he criticized the idea of shareholder value, saying that it resulted from a good business but should not be the focus. It was too late for the workers he laid off and certainly too late for the rest of corporate America that had become obsessed with shareholder value to the detriment of anyone else in the business.

The Federal Reserve and inflation policy continues to advantage assets and wealth over money derived from labor. The Fed wanted to fix the inflation and employment problems simultaneously. Rather than flowing into wages, inflation flowed into assets and industries where costs could not be quickly undercut. Greenspan thought lower goods prices would bridge the wage gap (the 2011 documentary *The Flaw* covers this brilliantly). Instead, the cost of everything not out-sourced skyrocketed, and the inflation had to go somewhere—it went into housing and assets.

Thomas Piketty, in his book *Capital*, was spot on. Wealth derived from assets would be more valuable than wealth derived from labor. I then theorized that this is because capital seeks a frictionless return. However, even this did not satisfy my curiosity about this problem. What had gone wrong with the country and the economy? I was always looking for the missing piece. It would be a documentary on Ronald Reagan's life that would give that missing piece. It had to do with white, college-educated, professional boomers. People who worked in white-collar professions were not unionized and didn't understand the importance of unions and how those high wages and stability held up the economy. They voted for their self-interest by voting for Reagan because they did not identify with their fellow workers. They didn't know their jobs were at risk in the coming decades, and no one knew their children would be entirely shut out of the labor market. It seemed like his message of "getting government off your back" and "gov-ernment is the problem" would solve the problems faced by stagfla-tion. The reality is that the desire for lower taxes, more money, and a chance to "get ahead" (in ways that might have been prevented by the economic structures of the New Deal) was more important than maintaining a middle-class life for people. The philosophy of "Why should I pay for the other guy?" began to prevail, and this simple act of avarice would undermine the greatest expansion of middle-class wealth in human history.

In 2011, as the Great Recession dragged on for its third year, the Obama recovery seemed to be stalled. The economy was still hemor-rhaging jobs, and the jobs being created tended to be low-wage service jobs. Obama complained about it then and made remarks about it post-presidency. For many millennials, Obama was the first president that they voted for. The earlier part of our cohort enjoyed the 2004 election with John Kerry and his swift boats. Obama rose to power in 2008 on the platform "hope and change." It seemed like America was headed for a new day. Horizons seemed brighter, and Chicago's young, popular Senator would lead the country in a new direction. John McCain represented the past, and Obama represented the future. Obama didn't have long to get ready for the big job. As voters went to the polls in 2008, the economy was falling apart under our collective feet. The Obama transition team was working with the Bush administration on TARP and other legislation as the two administrations tried to manage a broken economy. Two years later, all the Hope and Change from 2008 left the room as the Tea Party rose to power.

It is important to remember that many millennials grew up under odd political circumstances. For much of our generation, the Bush years were influential. We watched our government lie about evidence and cause a war. We saw how our country rushed to war after 9/11, and our young lives were changed forever.

It is also essential to know that it is not just Gen Z who suffered from school shootings. Columbine was shot up in 1999 when the tail end of Gen X and the earliest millennials were in school. The Virginia Tech University shooting happened when I was in college, and I remember how frightened everyone was. It seemed like everyone was just walking outside, not knowing what to do or say. The administration at my school granted students in positions of responsibility keycard access to buildings on campus so that they could take shelter in the event of a shooter. School shootings went from being rare to commonplace as millennials walked down the halls of high schools and colleges and into their youth. How frightening must it be for millennial parents to be handling this issue now, given the commonplace nature of school violence? They lived through it, and now their children are trained to handle themselves during an active shooter incident.

The following quote seems prescient given the context of understanding American politics since 1980. It has always stuck out to me. In 2017 (via Tumblr), Justin Flynn said:

> Millennials don't believe in democracy because we have never experienced it. In the United States, Democracy was repealed in 1976 with the Buckley v. Valeo Supreme Court decision. This contended that giving money to political parties was 'free speech' and could not be infringed. In the stroke of a pen, American Democracy was dead and replaced with plutocracy. The ability to vote can be powerful, but not nearly as powerful as the ability to bribe, and this decision legalized bribery and called it 'campaign contributions.'"
>
> Since then, virtually none of the after-inflation economic gains have been shared by Americans who are not high-earners, and voters' opinions have had zero effect on policy. By contrast, the views of donors have a very high correlation.
>
> Democracy has been dead since before any millennial was born, and every year, the corpse that bears its name redistributes more wealth from the middle and lower classes to the corrupt. Can you blame us for disdaining a system that has done nothing but steal from us?

Occupy Wall Street began in 2011 when the Tea Party, the ascendant protest movement, moved into its new congressional seats. The 2010 election had been a disaster for Democrats. Fresh on the heels of their achievement with the Affordable Care Act, the American electorate rewarded them with losing the House and the Senate the year following.

CHAPTER 19:

EAT THE RICH

A submission from Reddit:

33M, I graduated with a degree and worked retail during college. I spent at least three years working at a high-volume call center for 12 hours. Our HR was a bitch, and our boss never gave us benefits; meanwhile, I was still towing the "be loyal to your company" ideology lie. Come New Years I saw way more being turned over and bodies coming in, I didn't want to deal with the prospect of cleaning up a bunch of new people's mistakes so I left. Next job was another call center place but at $16 an hour. I helped clean up their website, introduced cool marketing ideas they enjoyed and even organized game nights. My immediate boss really liked me but he got busted for stealing product from the warehouse and another guy came in. He pretty much fired me (and the rest of the department) on the grounds of "multiple warnings" as well as failure to respond to a customer online. I had documented proof that said customer never got back to me and I challenged them to bring up any warnings they had on me (I had none). He said I could come back the next day to plead my case and I knew even if I got my job back I was "marked" and that any misstep I'd be out the door so I just filed for UI and showed EDD my evidence. They complied.

I spent at least a year bouncing between freelance jobs and working as an actor at a themed attraction. The co-workers were cool and the job fun but the pay was horrible. We all were part-time minus the managers, had to work holidays with no OT, and a number of reported sexual abuse cases were covered up with the guilty parties having no penalties. There were other incidents where actors were punched or had racist slurs yelled at them from the guests and management would not lift a finger to boot them out. It got so bad that a number of women employees left out of protest. I later learned that the company had a horrible reputation on various local casting websites and people all agreed to get in there, get your experience, then get out.

Without any senior experience, getting a job was hard but I lucked out as I got work in a (large corporation) mailroom through a staffing agency and got paid $17 an hour. Job was easy going, snacks were great and the conditions were pretty lax. I liked the pace and my co-workers but noticed that only 1/4 of the team were FTE and many of us were being paid way less than others. I found out one of the temps who got in before me and was there for over a year made 4 dollars LESS than meanwhile another guy who was from the same staffing agency got 4 dollars more. What really pissed me off was how the CEO and the company talked from both sides of their mouth saying "we're all Ohana" and "we're all family" with the CEO going on daytime TV saying how he wanted to abolish the pay gap, yet here we were all working for way less cause he used so many temp agencies. What was really insulting was the Christmas party, after being a part of the mail team, working much harder, finding packages and saving people's Christmas as they begged for packages to be found before they flew out on big week-long vacations (stuff we didn't get), with some of those packages housing clothes that they would wear TO the party. After all that BS, we could not attend that same party unless we were invited by a FTE. Over 18 months in, I reported an injury and had to go to rehab to fix my arm; that same month my contract was not renewed. A month later, I found another temp job working for (large retail chain), ironically I was treated better, got paid way more and while the job was only for 6 months, there were no pretensions of family. I hated losing the gig but at least they didn't put on a show of equality.

Which leaves me here, unemployed for over seven months. I'm trying to move into event management and marketing positions as that's what a lot of the volunteer work I've been doing is. However, people said I haven't been hired as because I'm not in their industry of choice, have no direct experience or haven't had the job enough to their liking. I managed a nationally recognized event that has expanded outside of CA on my own dime. I know I can do the job but people just see it as a fun hobby. I'm stuck in this weird holding pattern where I can only get free experience while my professional resume is just a string of random entry level jobs one after another. The job search has been hard as many of the company sites I go to, over half their openings say "senior" on it and that leaves me out of the running.

RICH BRUNCH

When President Franklin Roosevelt rose to power in 1932, his campaign program was straightforward: to get America out of the mess of the Great Depression that had already gone on for three years. At his inaugural address in March of 1933, he openly said that if things did not improve, he would not be afraid to ask Congress for "powers of sweeping executive action." FDR would use his coalition to get some sweeping executive powers, but he would also begin to pass the legislation forming the basis of the New Deal. One of the first pieces of legislation was ironically nicknamed the "Soak the Rich" bill. FDR raised taxes to their highest levels, ninety percent for the highest tax brackets, and he used that new revenue to pay for the largest intervention in the American economy in U.S. history. Fast forward eighty years, and it seems like, at least to millennials, it is time to soak the rich again.

Why many millennials want to eat the rich isn't a mystery. This impetus has been a slogan of the working classes for centuries. However, given the conditions under which many millennials have been forced to work, it is not a surprise that the anger has to go somewhere. Since the Great Depressions and the bailouts that followed, young people saw, between 2008 and the start of the pandemic, companies increasing share buybacks and dividends rather than increasing wages. Worse, the taxpayer was responsible for picking up the tab when the banks ran out of money through their mismanagement. By 2011, people were in the streets.

The anti-rich sentiment has only grown since the Occupy movement. The slogan "We are the 99 percent" began to echo in the streets of cities worldwide, decrying the seemingly increased inequality of our times and the politics of bailouts after the Great Recession.

Millennials have turned against capitalism, and it doesn't take long to find anti-capitalist sentiments on social media or even in the press. Since the 2008 crisis, more people have developed a much more negative view of capitalism. According to a 2018 Gallup poll that was widely reported, less than 45 percent of millennials approved of capitalism.

It was after 2008 that academics and others began turning a lens onto capitalism. Thomas Piketty wrote his great tome on capitalism, *Capital.* I even started my first book with two blistering essays on capitalism and the corporate aristocracy. Not since Karl Marx did so many people look at our modern economic system and ask pointed questions. Late-stage capitalism has become a passphrase for our current economic conditions. More people are starting to look at alternative lifestyles.

We know the cute, young, millennial couple doing #vanlife. Living in a van down by the river was once a sentence worse than death (per the season two Saturday Night Live sketch), but living in a van has become aspirational for millennials. Since the pandemic, though, living in a van with no permanent place has become not only passe but dangerous, given rising crime rates. But without COVID, it would have likely continued to be a tremendous trend. The pandemic still hasn't stopped some people from doing it anyway. If millennials can't afford a home, they may as well travel, right?

There is also a sense of daily humiliation, as in the story at the beginning of this chapter. Where people who have economic privilege exploit people without those same privileges for their own ends. It is not a surprise that capitalism and our present neoliberal economic system are not popular with most folks under 50.

Matthew Klein analyzed data from the U.S. Bureau of Economic Analysis and postulated that one of the biggest problems with the post-2008 economy was the complete lack of economic growth. In his article titled "Let's Overshoot," published on his Substack newsletter, *The Overshoot*, on February 17, 2021, he made the following commentary:

> The average American produced 2.2% more goods and services each year from the beginning of 1947 until the end of 2006. Despite violent business cycles and a range of countervailing forces, the U.S. economy always stayed within 8% of its stable long-term trend until the financial crisis. The defining feature of the crisis wasn't the severity of the initial hit to incomes and production but what happened next: nothing. There was no snapback. There was no "Morning in

America." The average American's real income didn't return to its pre-crisis level until mid-July 2013. The agonizingly slow growth after the crisis meant that U.S. output per person by the eve of the pandemic was 14% below where it would have been if the 1946-2006 trend had held steady. It was an enormous and costly undershoot. Put another way, the average American earned about $9,600 less in 2019 than reasonably expected before the financial crisis.

National income has been flowing to the wealthy as well. According to the Federal Reserve, millennials control only four percent of the national wealth, and two percent of that (according to the calculations of independent researchers) is owned entirely by Mark Zuckerberg. Even Gen X, with their eighteen percent share, is doing better than millennials, but neither generation compares to the fifty-five percent of baby boomers. It should be no surprise that millennials want to eat the rich: they have all the money.

Income is another area where statistics can be deceptive. On the one hand, "household income" is the highest it has ever been until you chop out the top ten percent of earners. Remove the top ten percent, and the average income drops, while household income does the same. The popular money website The Motley Fool in their article, "Are You Well Paid? Compare Your Income to the Average U.S. Income," reports that the "average U.S. income in 2023 was $114,500." However, they also say, "When the median is considerably lower than the average, it means that there are outliers on the top end. A few people who make a lot of money boost the average. The median income, $80,610 is a more accurate representation of typical household earnings."

SOCIALISM

One of the trends, tracking along with millennial disapproval of capitalism, is the rise of the approval of socialism. It should be noted right at the beginning that when most people under 40 say they approve of socialism, they do not think of the old Soviet Union, Venezuela, or Cuba; instead, they think of places like France or Scandinavian countries. These are places where democracy and capitalism co-exist with strong social safety nets, social support, low-cost education, and universal healthcare.

The internet here has played a role in the changing attitudes toward socialism. As younger people have interacted with others from overseas on social media and the problems with the American system, have been laid bare, young people in the U.S. look enviously at Europe, where education is low-cost or free, and healthcare is available to anyone without fear of a terrible bill. The U.S. is the only developed country with a for-profit healthcare system that can tie people into debt for years. Sites like GoFundMe and other fundraising sites are full of people panhandling on the internet for money to pay medical bills and setbacks. Donations have replaced the support that society should provide.

It is no surprise that the approval of socialism has increased for younger people who are tied down with student loan debt and who often must live without health insurance once they reach the age of 26. For those with chronic conditions or those who need medical attention, this can be an insurmountable problem. This is matched with fewer people getting health benefits from their employers. Although 188 million Americans get health insurance from their jobs, that leaves a gap of nearly two-thirds of the population. The Affordable Care Act has been a stopgap, and Medicaid expansion has helped, but these programs cannot match genuinely universal healthcare.

The popularity of Bernie Sanders on this point alone demonstrates how many people feel these social programs are necessary for a functioning and civilized society. This attitude stands at odds with the hyper-individualism of the neoliberal boomer politic.

CHAPTER 20:

Dating, Men's Rights, and PUA

On a nearly weekly basis, someone will post a graph on Twitter/X or write a think piece about how the younger generations just aren't having as much sex as they could or should be having. There has been a drop-off between Gen X and millennials and an even bigger drop-off between millennials and Gen Z.

In a study by co-led Tsung-chieh "Jane" Fu as part of the University of Indiana School of Public Health and published in the *Archives of Sexual Behavior*, the number of men (18-25) who have had sex in the last year (2018) dropped to its lowest level ever recorded with one in three reporting that they have not had sex in the previous year. The researchers took their data from the National Survey of Sexual Health and Behavior that the University conducts periodically.

My aunt has a cartoon on her fridge that says, "Trends come and go, but sex never goes out of style." It seems like sex has finally gone out of style. Problems with sex, dating, and the rise of the men's rights movement may have begun with millennials in the wake of the 2008 recession, but it has only grown and is now sucking in Gen Z.

The dating lives of millennials have been far different than their forebears. The most obvious change is the rise of the internet, which has become the primary way of meeting people. Rates of people meeting through friends have steadily declined since the 1990s, while the number of people meeting a love interest online has steadily grown.

This innovation in dating has been a loser for both men and women (in consideration of heterosexual relationships). Women are bombarded by all sorts of terrible messages, unsolicited pictures of an illicit variety, and often some of the most terrible human behavior on the internet. For men, online dating has become a contest of trying to get seen through the noise. This often leads to few matches. This new dynamic is primarily due to the fact that the internet has dramatically expanded pool of potential mates. Consider this: before online dating, people's pool of potential mates was relatively small because it was limited to their social circle. Due to time constraints, expanding that social circle wasn't necessarily easy.

Men, in particular, have been set adrift in this new dating environment. This is quite obvious on social media and through such channels as Joe Rogan's podcast, *The Joe Rogan Experience*. Men often became obsessed with going to the gym and working out to perfect the proper physique. The language of "alphas and betas" and "chads and stacys" has become standard terminology for the minority of men who enjoy dating success. A now viral article by the "Worst-Online-Dater" reported that "It was determined that the bottom 80% of men (in terms of attractiveness) are competing for the bottom 22% of women and the top 78% of women are competing for the top 20% of men. The Gini coefficient for the Tinder economy based on "like" percentages was calculated to be 0.58. This means that the Tinder economy has more inequality than 95.1% of all the world's national economies. In addition, it was determined that a man of average attractiveness would be "liked" by approximately 0.87% (1 in 115) of women on Tinder."

The article concludes with simple advice: If you're an average attractive guy, you're better off staying off the apps and going to bars or joining a recreation group.

And just like everything else in the United States, race influences dating. A 2021 article in PsyPost, an independent science news website, reported on a study about mobile apps dating. It found that "Dating on mobile apps has turned traditional dating on its head. A lot of the current research we have on how people meet romantic partners comes from relatively controlled settings—meeting through friends, at work, out in public, or online." The lead author was William J. Chopik, an associate professor and director of the Close Relationships Lab at Michigan State University.

Chopik continued, "The most consistent finding from our study is that, by far, people use very surface-level features to swipe on romantic partners. It's how attractive people are and, more surprisingly, the person's race. People of color experience a large penalty when navigating these dating apps—they're less likely to be swiped right on (i.e., chosen) controlling for how attractive they are."

The participants provided the researchers with demographic information such as their age, sex, race, whether they were in a relationship, and whether they were open to dating someone outside their race. They also completed assessments of attachment anxiety, sociosexuality, the Big Five personality traits, and self-esteem. However, these individual differences were primarily unrelated to dating choices.

"Also surprising is just how many things didn't matter! At least at this initial stage, it doesn't matter much who the person choosing is—their personality, how much they wanted short-term relationships/hook-ups, or even much about the people being chosen—how symmetric their face was, how they wore their hair," Chopik said. "What mattered most when swiping was how attractive the people were and whether they were from the same racial/ethnic group. It sheds light on the types of things that go into how people choose romantic partners in these settings."

Dating apps for women have been a source of sexual harassment. Police in the Australian state of New South Wales now work with Tinder's parent company to look at sexual assault and scan for sexual assault on the app. A 2021 *Wired* article reported that a 2019 survey by ProPublica and Columbia Journalism Investigations—one of the only articles ever to take this issue seriously—found that "more than a third of women said they were sexually assaulted by someone they had met through a dating app," and "of these women, more than half said they were raped." But when women try to report these incidents, many say the dating apps in question often don't even respond. In the #MeToo era, how are these companies still able to get away with this?"

Dating apps can be as problematic for women as they are for men, just in different ways, as we can see. For men, dating apps are pointless unless they are attractive, and for women, they are a cesspool of the worst behavior of humanity delivered into their collective pockets. The flurry of poor conversation skills, genital photography, and tawdry behavior has women fleeing from the apps.

The standards for sex and dating have changed along with the economics. Women are no longer dependent on men for economic security. This is very good. However, women now expect much more from men regarding romance. It is no longer enough to be merely a provider—a man must also bear the "emotional labor" of the relationship and the household. Fathers are taking a more prominent role in rearing children, which mirrors a trend throughout the developed world. The expectations are rising as women expect men to do more, be more, express emotional intelligence, and be more than just a paycheck because they don't need their money nearly as much as they did in the past. It is essential to be mindful that these expectations are not negative. They merely reflect the times. However, this factor has again upended the dating market.

These trends mean that the primary source of meeting a potential mate for millennials is an arena that is fraught with difficulty, stress, and, in the most extreme cases, long-term trauma. Standards have changed, and that has left people feeling lonely and dissatisfied. We now talk of the loneliness epidemic. These trends take on a different take when we look at LGBT relationships.

Dating apps are far more popular in the LGBTQIA community, and users report getting into more relationships through apps than do their heterosexual counterparts. Pew Research investigated this and found that fifty-five percent of LGBTQ people were asked to report using a dating app, and twenty-one percent reported finding a marriage or long-term relationship using dating apps. This outpaces heterosexual couples by twenty percent for use and nearly double for long-term relationships or marriage. However, despite their increase in use, dating apps for LGBT people have their difficulties. Violence and assault can still occur. This is well-known in the lesbian community, and some incidences have made headlines. For gay men, dating apps can be a minefield of racism, internalized homophobia, and unfair stereotyping based on feminine characteristics. Body shaming can be common as well. In short, to quote 1980s pop star, Pat Benatar, "Love is a battlefield."

Back in the heterosexual world, many men have begun promoting the dating hierarchy idea. It is simple and based on some data. The trope goes that eighty percent of women chase after twenty percent of men and that dating today has no point if you don't fall in the twenty percent "Chad" category (square jawline, fit body, good skin, attractive). A new class of dating grifters has popped up to counter these issues in modern dating. The so-called pick-up artists promise to teach men how to run "day games" or pick women up in public during the day using confidence skills and basic conversation. Then there's also the "night game," which involves exploring bars and clubs, which is more treacherous but often more successful. The next great hookup is just around the corner if you can fix your fashion, make the most of your looks, have a decent body, and have overwhelming confidence. Do these methods work? That is unclear, but the people charging guys to learn how to do this are doing well.

Dating has been a minefield for every generation. I've heard the stories from my 85-year-old Nana about small-town dating in the 1950s. I've heard stories from my mother as well. Those stories alone cross two separate generations. Finding a life partner and mate has never been easy (except for arranged marriages, to some degree). Still, the modern dating environment has been particularly toxic for millennials and now Gen Z.

Then, there is the MGTOW movement. MGTOW stands for "Men Going Their Own Way." Starting with some of the darker aspects of the internet, thanks to social media, this movement has grown in interest. Known chiefly for its blatant misogyny, MGTOW has a simple mandate for men: walk away from women. Have sex with them if you must, but don't date them or marry them. The arguments for this kind of lifestyle usually include how men are abused by the court system in divorce (especially if children are involved) and observations, however true or false they might be, that women use men like tissues and will leave any man if they can get a better deal. None of this is new to the many books and internet websites devoted to dating. These complaints can be read about going back centuries, even when the cultural pressures toward marriage were very different. As we've seen from the studies from the dating sites, the deck is stacked and not in the favor of men.

Still further is the "incel" situation. Incel is short for "involuntary celibate." There is a fringe group of men who believe that sex is intentionally being held back from them. They desire sex and the company of women and cannot seem to access it, making them involuntary celibates. Incels and inceldom are not taken seriously, but the reality is that young men are getting lonelier. Professor Scott Galloway has often been speaking on this recently. Even before the pandemic, young people were spending less time together socially, and sex and dating have dropped by half since 2020 in recent studies, as reported in *The New York Times* and also reported by the Surgeon General and the U.S. Department of Health and Human Services.

Incel has become a byword for a "loser" guy who can't get a date and won't put in any effort to make himself more appealing to women. People will blame everything from personality to looks, and this commentary goes both ways. In online forums, guys will bemoan everything from their hairline to their facial ratios. Similarly, other content creators, usually female, will complain that too many guys aren't over six feet, do not make six figures, or do not have the proper male append-age of at least six inches. This is another area where the dialogue about men and women is completely broken and serves no one. Incels have become modestly politically active, especially in the Republican party, and organizations like the Proud Boys—as well as the cult of person-ality surrounding pop psychologist Jordan Peterson—have spoken to these disaffected young men.

The rest of the men's rights movement is between the pick-up art-ists and the MGTOW guys. The most notable force for this is A Voice for Men, a website run by Paul Elam, whom I have interviewed. Men certainly face some issues, specifically in the modern context. Family and divorce courts are some of the country's most unfriendly spaces for men. This trend has begun to shift, but only slightly.

There has also been the rise of the #metoo movement. The perva-siveness of rape culture certainly is worthy of attack, but the knock-on effect is that innocent dating interactions between young people can often become major legal issues. The standard now is that the mere allegation of impropriety is nearly as good as proof. There is always vitriol and accusations when the initial claims are made and much less hubbub when someone is proven innocent. I'm young enough to have seen this story unfold before my eyes. However, there have been notable cases like the Stanford Lacrosse team whose members were accused of rape, and as it turns out, there was nothing to it. This does not save their academic careers, though, and will follow them for the rest of their lives and adversely affect them forever.

An argument can be made that a few false accusations hardly out-weigh the good that is done by having more and more victims come forward. This is a tradeoff—but hardly a fair one for the people being accused.

Sex and dating have become a complicated environment where online dating is complex, young people are afraid to date, and there are shifting social mores around dating—particularly around age gaps in dating. It isn't a wonder that so many people, both men and women, are deciding to check out of dating altogether. This has led people like Elon Musk and others to lament America's falling birthrate and how few people are having babies. Millennials on social media will decry the cost of housing and childcare as to why they haven't produced more children. Millennials are starting to have some children, but not nearly enough to replace themselves, and Gen Z has hardly begun to add to those numbers.

Economically, programs like Social Security and Medicare face major financial pitfalls, with more older adults drawing from the system than young people putting into it. People are living longer, too, which strains these systems even more. It is not a throw-away concern, and the stability of social programs is a concern throughout the developed world as populations are set to shrink rather than expand.

As millennials reach the tail end of their childbearing years, the time to fix their low birth rate was nearly ten years ago, and given the economics of the time, it is no secret why many chose to either delay children or not have them at all. For those who have had children, the rising costs have been crushing, with little relief in sight.

CHAPTER 21:

MARRIAGE, HOUSES, AND CHILDREN

A submission from Reddit:

> I'm a lawyer. Trying to be one anyway. An aspect no one talks about is how millennials take care of a parent who become disabled are impacted by that disability.

> I graduated law school in 2013. My mother developed early onset dementia around this time and gave away hundreds of thousands of dollars to scammers. I could not spend the time I needed to pass the bar exam and had to help her and manage her estate. It was hard, a situation that was compounded by the fact that I had a complex relationship with her as she was horrifically negligent and abusive to me as a child. Still, I took care of her anyway as my parents were divorced and my father wanted nothing to do with her.

> As a law graduate, without passing the bar I had no job opportunities and started lifeguarding again, a nearly minimum-wage job. I briefly worked as a law clerk, but the attorney was too incompetent to continue working with. I couldn't relocate either as I had to stay in the area for my

mother as I was her legally appointed guardian. It took a few years for things to settle down (my grandfather had congestive heart failure during this time too, but he thankfully survived and fully recovered) and have the time to fully devote myself to studying. I passed shortly thereafter.

I found that passing the bar exam made no difference. There were no jobs available for new attorneys. I was laughed out of a few interviews because I had no experience. It was a very frustrating time. I realized I had to volunteer (i.e., work for free) in order to get that experience.

I have since volunteered for several years in order to find employment. I haven't had any luck yet, but I have been getting more interview requests. In the interim I obtained an LLM degree in taxation both to enhance my resume and prepare me to switch careers if necessary. I am also still relying on my supportive father to cover my rent. Hopefully it all pans out one day and I can land a job. Until it does, I'm still volunteering and lifeguarding...

HOUSING IN CRISIS

It is no secret that millennials have struggled to get married, have children, and buy houses. The millennials' plight with housing will be discussed further. Still, it is essential to note that the cost of housing, education, and healthcare has risen steadily over the past four decades and as millennials have become adults. Many get caught in a catch-22 situation where they can afford a higher rent than their mortgage but cannot save for a down payment.

In early 2023, there was a TikTok trend of people talking about how difficult it is to buy a house. Social media is littered with stories of people who couldn't buy houses even with good incomes. It all comes down to price. My parents bought their home in 1993 for $104,000 (or so), which is now worth four times that amount. It's an amount of money that is simply out of reach for the average person now.

While it is not impossible to get married without buying a house, many of the two are linked together, especially once children are involved. Now, it is much more common (fifty-one percent rent, according to *The New York Times*) to rent your residence rather than own, which is a significant reversal from just twenty years ago.

However, it's not all bad. A recent article from *Business Insider* (April 2023) stated: "This building boom (in the 1970s) helped drive home-ownership—more than half of boomers owned a home by the age of 30, compared with 48% of Gen Xers and 42% of millennials. Boomers have also sustained their home buying activity longer than their predecessors, who were more likely to settle into one home. The share of recent buyers who were 60 years and older grew 47% from 2009 to 2019, which means millennials, 'face more competition from their parents' and grandparents' generations than their predecessors did,' a Zillow study found." Gen Z is already outpacing millennials in home buying at the same age because of the post-pandemic squeeze for labor that has boosted their wages. Millennials did not have any such boost coming out of 2008, and wages will never recover for those of us who graduated in a recession. This means a new renting underclass has developed, which will rent into their old age and create a retirement and housing crisis.

MARRIAGE

When it comes to marriage, millennials tend to eschew the institution. In 2013, only twenty-six percent of millennials were married compared to people the same age in 1980 (according to the National Association of Women REO Brokerages, a real estate group). The NAWRB credits the lower marriage rate to simple economics. Some people choose to cohabitate, and that arrangement has steadily risen. However, given what we know about dating in the previous chapter, it is also no secret why rates of marriage are down—dating and sex are a complete disaster for the vast majority of people. If people aren't dating and having sex, they certainly aren't getting married and forming households.

These conditions have had their backlash. The online discourse to encourage women to be "trad" or "submissive" has begun in earnest response to this long trend of eschewing marriage. Most of the ire about marriage is focused on women, not men—as if it is women's fault that marriage and birth rates are down.

COMMUNITY

One of the sacrifices of our present economic system is community, which is the foundation of strong relations and families. Neoliberal economics prioritizes the individual and their choices over what benefits society as a whole. Economically, this approach has led to financialization and economic growth but has come at the cost of rising income inequality and stagnant wages, along with the attendant erosion of community and the social fabric it sustains.

Despite all this, millennials are known for their collaborative nature and how well they work together and in groups, much in contrast to Gen X or Gen Z. Somehow, within the context of neoliberalism, that has been the dominant political force for their lives since millennials were taught from a young age to work together, and they love to work in groups.

One of the markers of this generation is a distinct lack of community. Community is a struggle for many because our world isn't built for a community like it was in the past. Unions and other social service organizations have been on a decline. Given the hours worked, there is also less time to pursue these efforts. The average work week is well over 40 hours—47.5 hours, according to the Federal Reserve—and with many people working second jobs or side hustles, far less time is left for community.

Piled on top of that is the dominance of the nuclear family and the lack of extended families. One of the trends I've noticed among my friends, as they started to have children, is how many moved closer to their families. It was usually her family, but today's young mothers have recognized the need for grandparents and extended families to help care for children. This is a good thing for parents and children, given how much energy we require parents to pour into their children these days. The parents of young children need all the help they can get, and extended families are just what is required. This is another example of millennials working together collaboratively to achieve their goals.

The reality is that these things are all linked together. Getting married, having children, and buying a home to raise a family are essential life milestones afforded to the generations previously and are simply not available to the mass of millennials. The housing situation, both in rising rents and house prices, has advantaged those who own homes or can get help to buy homes from their families, but it has disadvantaged anyone trying to earn enough money to buy their own homes. Given these costs, it is no wonder people aren't dating, getting married, and starting families. In 2022, the American birth rate dropped below replacement levels for the first time since the end of World War II, and the online discourse immediately blamed everything and everyone but the obvious: Family life is expensive, and if people can't afford to live by themselves, most are not going to bring children into the equation. As geopolitical scientist and demographic fetishist Peter Zeihan remarks, "Adults aren't stupid; children are expensive pets, so they have fewer of them."

CHAPTER 22:

MILLENNIALS ARE JUST ADULT CHILDREN

A submission from Reddit:"

I'll share my story. Hopefully, this isn't too late. I know this was posted a few weeks ago.

I'm a 28 year old male. I graduated with a bachelor's degree a handful of years ago—made good grades and even turned down an opportunity to stay in academia, which now I believe was a huge mistake. At the time, I didn't think landing a professional job post-graduation was going to be that difficult of a feat, neither did my parents.

I started job searching months before I graduated, but I had no success—no call backs. At this point, I started to slowly realize the situation I was in. I was also astonished at the lack of entry-level jobs in my area.

Upon graduation, it took me six months to land a job. My first job post-graduation was working as a teaching assistant in a special needs classroom making $11 an hour. This job was completely unrelated to my degree, but it was a job and somewhat more respectable than working retail. I thought it would help me land something better.

After I landed that job, I started getting calls back for entry-level corporate gigs a few months later—stuff like customer service rep, claims trainee, inside sales rep, etc. I hardly ever made it past the phone screen though. When I did get an actual interview, my lack of experience was cited by every interviewer as my key weakness. Apparently, I didn't have enough experience to be qualified to talk to people on the phone.

I remember conducting a phone interview with an HR assistant about 12 months post-graduation for a customer service job at a Fortune 50 company that paid $14 an hour. She flat-out told me that I was lucky to have even made it to this point in the interview process—that I was competing with hundreds of applicants, most of which were in the same boat as me (no experience and a degree). She kept asking me if I knew anyone at the company—that that was probably the only way I would get hired, an internal reference due to the amount of applicants. I didn't know anyone. I passed the phone interview, went into their corporate headquarters for an in person interview. The interviewer seemed immediately disinterested in me as a candidate, and I immediately started sensing that the position had already been filled, and I was just there to make some bizarre candidate quota. I wasn't extended an offer.

After a year working as a teaching assistant, I still wasn't anywhere professionally. I toyed with the idea of getting an MA in Education so that I could work as a teacher, but getting certified to teach in my state would require two years of additional education followed by six months of unpaid "student teaching" in the public school system—then I would be eligible to apply for a license. That didn't seem reasonable for a job starting at less than $35,000 a year.

At this point, I was frustrated with my professional job search, went to a local staffing agency, and I got a temp-to-hire position as a general laborer at a local manufacturing plant. I was now making $14.50 an hour, and I had just enough income to finally move out of my parents' house. I excelled in the position, got hired on full-time direct, and I worked my way into a machine operating position.

All this time, I was still job searching. I was eventually offered a position at BCBS as a claims trainee, but they were only offering $12 an hour with only 32 hours a week guaranteed. That wasn't remotely enough to support myself on so I had to turn it down.

Eventually, I landed a job as Manufacturing Management Trainee in a different city. I moved cities, but soon found out that the position was a bit of a bait and switch—a more apt title for the position would have been "Supervisor Trainee." I was hired in with three other guys, and I soon found out that the company had over hired for the position, and they only needed one person for the role—one guy was fired within two months of hire, and another guy was permanently relegated to a QC position because the VP didn't think he "smiled enough." Mind you, these are both college grads with business management degrees.

I eventually moved into the supervisor role, but I shortly left the company thereafter. I didn't see any room for advancement, the workplace culture was toxic, and the pay was low with little room for advancement. For example, I was given a $1 "raise" when they moved me into the supervisor role. I was told this was a raise. I later found out that everyone that works on second shift gets a $1 shift-differential tacked onto their hourly pay—it really wasn't a raise.

When I left, the VP tried to convince me to stay by telling me that he had an aging workforce, and there'd be potential room for advancement when people retired. That was my counter-offer—not here's a raise or we're willing to give you additional responsibilities and train you on the business side of our operations, but that there might be room for advancement when people retire.

I am now living back in my hometown, and I am working as a Pastry and Bread Baker at a local grocery store making $13 an hour. I had originally thought this would just be a temporary job until I could find better work, but with how the economy is right now, it's looking like this is going to become my permanent role for a while. No one is hiring.

I really don't know what to do with my life anymore. I'm living in a not so good part of town, because it's all I can afford. My employment history is a bit scattered. I'm nearing 30, and I have no savings; I have about $3,000 in my checking account and another $2,000 in investments. I haven't even had a company provided 401k since I left the public school system. I don't see a lot of hope for my future. I don't see myself ever being able to afford having kids, and quite honestly, I wouldn't want to try and raise a family in an apartment complex in a high-crime area. I'm not financially stable enough to even consider marriage—that's a pipe dream at this point. I've pretty much just stopped dating due to financial stress—I can't afford it, and my lack of income completely destroyed my last relationship. Women expect you to buy shit for them, and stuff as little as birthday and Christmas gifts were leading to fights, e.g., "I don't care if it's your birthday; I can't afford to buy you a $400 necklace." That's basically half of my entire week's pay.

It isn't surprising that people in their 30s are somewhat childlike. Our society has excluded many from advancing to a brighter future. There's no West to conquer. We can't send people somewhere new: we have to fix our problems. There are many ways to initiate young people into society. We don't have many rituals to do this in modern secular society. Some of our rituals are learning how to drive, getting married or having a long-term relationship, getting a good job, and having children, among the few. In sacred settings, it's the responsibility in the community. In clubs, it can be election to an office. In politics, it's an increase in political power.

America has genuinely failed to initiate millennials into society, leaving many behind or clinging to the side of the pool. It is not the environment that engenders a deep engagement with greater society and gives most people a sense of place in the world. This sense of place within the greater human community is essential.

Socially, this has manifested itself in our culture. The popularity of Marvel movies and the general acceptance of what was once considered "nerd" or "geek" culture has further reinforced this juvenile state. This current phenomenon is quite different than the Youth Quake of the 1960s. It is not uncommon for people in their 20s, 30s, and beyond to still collect Pokemon cards. Remember the great Pokemon Go craze of 2016? The new gaming phenomenon was not just children going into the world; grown people were playing along, too. This would have been unheard of decades ago. But much like their Japanese cousins, millennials buy the aspirational things they can afford. Oddly, young Japanese people will wait outside Louis Vuitton for a new bag while they could use those resources elsewhere. The logic is simple: if people can't buy homes and an adult life, at least they can own a rare Pokemon card or a limited edition LV bag.

Millennials didn't see any reason to give up their hobbies as they grew older. Video games are ubiquitous. Everyone plays them and enjoys them. Athletes, who wouldn't have been caught dead near a gaming console in an earlier generation, are now punching out other men to get their hands on a PS5. Games like Madden, NBA2K, Call of Duty, and Grand Theft Auto have become cultural tour-de-forces, complete with memes and pop culture references. If you had told anyone in the mid-1990s that this would be the case, we would have laughed in your face at the very suggestion.

However, this all does represent a shift. The line between childhood, adolescence, and adulthood has grown blurry. Terms like "adulting" have entered the national lexicon as millennials learned to navigate such things as making their own doctor's appointments, scheduling their cars for service, and other mundane life tasks that were once considered normal. Now, those "not fun" and "boring" tasks have been lumped into the unfunny category of adulting. Older people would scream out, "but that's just life!" For millennials, the necessity to do these things, pick up a telephone, and make an actual call (oh, horror of horrors) represents something else. We are somehow divorced from the expected transition to adulthood. For millennials, adulthood is not something to be embraced; it is to be merely endured.

I think this primarily concerns the lack of special privileges of adulthood. It certainly isn't what it used to be. For the under-45 set these days, it's an ever-rising cost of living, inflation, low wages, and figuring out how to survive with no clear path to any sort of stability or expectation of safety. The twenty-first century has been marked with crisis after crisis that has rocked the world at every level. Millennials and now Gen Z are navigating these changes without being able to have any real effect on the earth or to navigate the problems. The boomers have remained firmly in charge, so the generational conflict has often taken on a parent-child tone, especially in online spaces. But even the discourse around these topics that has gone on since the late aughts has been a tussle of think pieces on popular websites telling millennials to grow up while younger people have gently (and sometimes not so gently) complained that they simply cannot.

Alicia Elliot stated it perfectly in a 2018 Maclean's article: "We've become a generation of Cinderellas, told to wait for a glass slipper that no longer exists." Her article was titled "Directionless and Lost." She offers hope at the end of the article, stating that at least millennials will find their path. But are we finding that path, or are we merely surviving while waiting for the other shoe to drop?

As we have learned from previous chapters about dating, sex, love, and marriage, the entire market has been turned upside down, leaving significant numbers of people uncoupled. Sex has finally gone out of style with people, and the latest crisis is the falling American birth rate. Blame is thrown on birth control, low testosterone levels in modern men, and other boogeymen that Alex Jones and other right-wing commentators bring up. The problem is far deeper.

SOCIAL MEDIA AND THE PERFECT LIFE

The arrival of social media in our society has changed culture, life, and attitudes in ways that can only be compared to mass media in their scope. Radio brought music and stories into people's homes. They no longer had to go to the theater or the cafe to hear a story. Television did one better, bringing the magic of movies and programs into people's living rooms. The writing about the arrival of television was decidedly dystopian. Newton N Minow, in his speech to the National Association of Broadcasters in 1961, declared television to be a "vast wasteland." He went on to say, "When television is good, nothing— not the theater, not the magazines or newspapers—nothing is better."

But when television is bad, nothing is worse. I invite each of you to sit down in front of your own television set when your station goes on the air and stay there for a day without a book, without a magazine, without a newspaper, without a profit and loss sheet or a rating book to distract you. Keep your eyes glued to that set until the station signs off. I can assure you that what you will observe is a vast wasteland.

You will see a procession of game shows, formula comedies about totally unbelievable families, blood and thunder, mayhem, violence, sadism, murder, western bad men, western good men, private eyes, gangsters, more violence, and cartoons. And endlessly, commercials—many screaming, cajoling, and offending. And most of all, boredom. True, you'll see a few things you will enjoy. But they will be very, very few. And if you think I exaggerate, I only ask you to try it.

I can only imagine what Minow would think of social media. If television were a vast wasteland, then social media would be a lower pit of desolation. It's a world of arguments, filtered selfies, and a never-ending highlight reel of seemingly unreal people living unreal lives and doing unreal things. While television programming was determined by authentic people in offices in New York and Los Angeles, social media is the sum total content of everyone uploading their profound, banal, and ordinary thoughts, pictures, and video constantly onto seven platforms (Facebook, Instagram, Tik Tok, Twitter/X, Pinterest, Reddit, YouTube) controlled by roughly six companies. These are just the American platforms. Add up the other platforms in other countries, especially China, and dozens exist. The feed of that prodigious amount of content is then curated, not by people, but by algorithms designed by a handful of engineers in California. These algorithms, much like their broadcasting forebears, focus not on the public good or the good of the users but on what will generate engagement. TV-chased ratings. Social media chases engagement. Engagement on a platform means that the user will engage and do two important tasks: generate sales data and click on ads that generate income. Social media companies can then sell their users' ads and data to target better ads. This has been enormously profitable.

The effect on millennials and their Gen Z cousins has been catastrophic. Depression and suicide among millennials have risen dramatically in the past decade. "The suicide rate among people aged 10 to 24 increased fifty-six percent between 2007 and 2017," according to the U.S. Centers for Disease Control. The picture is worse for Gen Z. The links between social media and depression itself are weak. In a cross-sectional article for the *International Journal of Adolescence and Youth*, the results of several studies were reported by Betul Keles, Niall McCrae & Annmarie Grealish in an article entitle, "A systematic review: the influence of social media on depression, anxiety and psychological distress in adolescents." It was found that social media was a mixed bag that strengthened some social bonds but also was detrimental to health because it could cause depression symptoms and other health issues due to the sedentary nature of the activity. The article also cited the comparison aspect of social media as a danger. Still, it was admitted that people who used social media and reported strong social bonds were better off than those with weak ones.

For millennials, social media, as we know it today, arrived while most were in college or in their early 20s. Myspace and Friendster, which predated Facebook, never had the cultural influence that modern social media platforms have today. Mark Zuckerberg, a millennial, was in college at Harvard and wanted a faster way to meet girls. Myspace had become a cluttered, HTML-heavy platform of custom pages and music played when you visited a profile and custom backgrounds. Facebook was clean and fresh, allowed no profile customization, and delivered the latest posts from all your friends right into your newsfeed. You added your "friends" to your account. When pages were launched, brands could do the same thing. First, we were fans and could "like" their pages. If you liked a status, you could press the like button and move on. It didn't matter what the post was about. The breadth and depth of human emotion were reduced to whether you did or did not "like" a post.

Facebook has since tried to fix this with seven reaction buttons, but the effect of emotional reduction is the same. Several girls in college broke down in tears because someone failed to like an update or, worse yet, someone "liked" something they shouldn't have. If you went through a break-up, your most powerful tool to express your displeasure was to unfriend them. Even a row with a friend, if severe enough, might earn them an unfriending. If you made up with them later, you could refriend them. We've invented a new language to discuss these platforms and how we behave on them. All the while, Facebook and the others have quietly collected the data on their users and sold it to anyone buying and continued to employ the most brilliant people in the country to find out how to keep its two billion global users engaged on the platform and scrolling, clicking, and making them more money through ads and data.

What is even worse about social media is that many people have become addicted to seeing the seemingly perfect life of others and then comparing themselves to this highlight reel. Even as older millennials approach 40, the people who lamented "likes" in college are now lamenting the family with more perfect children, the better car, or the better vacation. Keeping up with the Joneses on your block is no longer good enough. Now you're keeping up with the Joneses on every block, everywhere in the country, and sometimes the entire world. You would be correct if you think this might make some people feel perpetually inadequate. The constant influx of information from nearly everywhere has allowed people to find out about media, people, and entertainment that they might not otherwise have discovered. Still, it has also made life just seem so inadequate. What's a good meal unless you can produce a good picture for Instagram? What is an excellent vacation without creating the requisite social media material? Life and the business of living has been reduced to how it can look on social media. This had a tremendous influence on millennials in their 20s and even now.

In the years after the recession, millennials took different paths on a class basis. Those lucky enough to have wealthy parents who could assist them financially to move out could post splashy pics of their new apartments or houses. The rest of us living at home in the basement or a house with a small room and five roommates could only scroll with envy.

Those same people could also travel to exotic destinations and take even more dramatic pics. More than one Instagram feed in 2014 was filled with pictures of their next international ticket or tropical pictures from Bali. Others still filled their Instagram feeds with images of their latest road trip or pictures of their glamorous life living out of a van in stunning locations around North America. For those unable to participate in this new take on how to spend their

20s, a new phrase was coined for the feeling of FOMO—fear of missing out. In a generation set adrift with few options on what to do in a moribund job economy and shut out of housing and relationships, millennials rewrote what your 20s meant. Boomers dropped acid, went to Woodstock, protested Vietnam, fought in Vietnam, and then bought a house and raised kids. Gen X was on the career path and slaved away in corporate America. Millennials put on a Valencia filter and hopped on a flight to Bali, but only if they could afford it. For the rest, they stayed with parents and friends, shared situations, worked in terrible retail, warehouse, and food jobs, and posted pics of their crazy weekends while scrolling by looking at how it seemed like life was passing them by. Is it a mystery why millennials felt a Jimmy Carter-esque malaise? In the years before social media, you only had to worry about what you saw on TV, and you only had to compare yourself with the people in your town or on your side of town. Now, the comparison has gone nationwide and global.

Millennials are the generation that tried to win the system and "have it all" with the perfect life, but social media seems to have made that nearly impossible. Is the restaurant expensive enough? Is the food good enough? Is the outfit the best and most expensive? Are you wearing the right brands? The comparison goes on and on. It is no longer good enough to have a good Christmas at home or with family—is the tree good enough for Instagram?

This has hit American society right at its heart. Americans are an aspirational bunch. We want to do better than our parents and for our children to do better than us, and social media has poured gasoline on that desire. Rather than being content with where we are or having a limited view of comparison, we aspire to be everyone all at the same time. The human brain is not equipped to deal with this kind of information. This has resulted in higher rates of depression and suicide. Millennials have been hit with a double whammy of extreme aspirations while unable to achieve most of them in measurable terms.

CHAPTER 23:

HOUSING, FOOD AND TRANSPORTATION

A submission from Reddit:

Back at the start of 2016, I was working at an electronics/ appliance store. I'd only been there for a few months, but it wasn't my first retail gig. It was pretty well par for the course as far as my prior jobs were concerned: 32-40 hours a week, barely enough pay to get by on, deeply unsatisfying in almost every regard. I didn't have it in me to manage a second job, and since I didn't have a car at the time I was getting around on foot, by bike, or by bus. Uber and Lyft hadn't really taken off at that point, at least not in my part of the U.S. My roommates and I supplemented our income as best we could: selling plasma, working odd jobs for family and friends, little one-time gigs here and there. Depending on the week we were being threatened with eviction, or our water had been shut off, or our power. We lived off whatever food we could scrounge together. More than once, we'd be without power for a day or two while we waited on paychecks to clear or tried to scrounge together enough cash to pay the minimum fee to have it reconnected. The summer of 2016, we were without power for a week. We had to do all our cooking off of a charcoal grill, spent our free time in the garage with the door open since the house itself was a sweltering mess during the day. Even at night it wasn't great. Our showers were cold, and once the sun went down, there wasn't really enough light to do anything.

I was at the end of my rope then. I'd run myself ragged trying to make things work, but there was just never enough cash to go around. A friend of mine kept trying to sell me on joining up with the automotive factory in town, said his dad made good money there, that there was opportunity. I didn't exactly jump on it at first, but eventually I started looking into the details. The money was good, and they even had an on-site branch of a local college. If you went through one of their offered courses, the company would foot the bill for your education. I told myself that would be my ticket to something better, that I'd only be at the factory long enough to get my degree. As far as I could tell, the only downside was you had to start as a Temp, but everything I'd heard made it pretty clear that most temps got shifted to Full Associates within a year. I figured I didn't have anything to lose, so I signed on. Temps got insurance through the agency, and I hadn't had health insurance for about two years at that point, so I was pretty keen to get myself looked at by a proper doctor, pay a visit to a dentist, all that jazz.

I still didn't have a car at this point, and the factory was about ten miles away from my home in the city. Only one bus route got you close to it, and even then it was still two miles from the last stop on the line to the factory's grounds. Naturally, though, the bus ran on a schedule that made it problematic at best and impossible to use for my purposes at the worst. I'd made up my mind though, I was doing this. I left the house three hours before my shift every single day, and I walked the full ten miles in most days. Sometimes, if I had the cash, I took the bus as far as I could. Sometimes other coworkers saw me on the way and picked me up.

You may be wondering why I didn't carpool. Well, I didn't know anyone at the plant. Even after I got to know people, I never asked for help from them. I couldn't bring myself to do it. In my experience, no one ever did anything for free: ask for help and you were in someone's debt, end of story. I'd walk in, work my full shift, then walk back out, every day. I was used to doing a lot of walking, but I only had one pair of shoes: very old, very well worn down work boots from Red Wing. They had been through two long years of wear and tear, the tread on them was practically gone, and the inserts had basically fallen to pieces (which I had kept held together by duck tape). My feet hurt so much by the time I got home every night, I couldn't even get up the stairs to my room until I'd taken my boots off and sat for a while.

My job at that time wasn't a difficult one, I delivered parts from the loading docks to their place in our warehouse. The money was better than I'd ever made elsewhere, but because of all the debts I had to pay off, my situation didn't really change much. The health Insurance offered by the temp agency was bare bones, minimal stuff: It'd cover you for a trip to the ER, took a bite out of the price of prescriptions, but even with what I was making I really couldn't afford it. I needed every damn penny I could get, and the ACA wasn't offering me anything better or more affordable. So I said 'Fuck Obamacare,' swallowed the fees he forced upon the working poor, and did without insurance.

About two months into my time at the plant, one of my roommates tried to kill himself. He was family, and I got the call towards the end of my shift. My mom had basically blown up my phone with a bunch of panicky texts and phone calls, asking me where I was, why I wasn't answering. Being the narcissist she was, mom preferred to be uselessly melodramatic rather than give me any useful information. My boss let me leave early since we were almost done anyway, and my brother picked me up at the plant. Since I was working nights, we spent the whole night at the hospital waiting on my roommate's parents, who lived about four hours away, to get to the hospital and see their son.

I didn't get any sleep, and I had to walk back into work the following day. Temps only got two excused days off for the entire year. Even taking one unexcused day would tank your attendance and put you in their disciplinary program, which meant you were taken off the hiring list for a year, bare minimum, until your attendance came back up to the plant's 98% standard. Emotionally, I was just...dead inside. I couldn't muster much more than a few words to answer a question, and mostly I just kept to myself. I didn't want to be there, but with only two excused absences for the entire rest of the year, I didn't have a choice. It was work, or put off being hired just to get some sleep. I powered through a ten hour shift, and by the time I got done I was so delirious I was jumping at shadows. I don't even really remember getting home, I just remember waking up the next day still in my work clothes.

So that sucked. Everything that came after sucked too.

We were now down a man, so me and the other roommate had to pick up the slack on all the bills, and rent. I went from making enough money to squirrel away a little chunk of emergency cash right back to struggling just to keep the damn lights on. The roommate who tried to commit suicide was placed in a facility for about two months, and even after he came back...well. There's a lot of baggage there. It took him forever to find a new job, and we basically had to support him the whole way. We made it, but it was rough. I'm honestly amazed we didn't kill each other sometimes. We managed to make it a few months without another crisis.

Eventually things stabilized, but financially I'd lost a lot of ground and our landlord flat out refused to renew our lease. Those rat bastards even called us a week before our lease was up to tell us we had 24 hours to vacate the premises. We didn't have money for a lawyer, since we'd spent all our cash on getting a new place set up, so I burned one of my two excused days off, one roommate got a moving van, and between the three of us we cleared out our house and moved in the span of a day. And yes, I did pull another ten hour shift with no sleep. After my first year at the plant, I was getting really anxious about getting hired by the company. I checked with my HR rep on a monthly basis, to see how much closer I was to getting in. As we passed the one-year mark, they just kept telling me: "Should be any month now, any month." I got moved to a different part of the plant shortly after my one-year anniversary as a temp. The place I got moved to was much closer to the start of the production line. It was hotter, and I had to wear a bunch of PPE that made it even worse. The tasks I had to perform were much more physically demanding, but I managed to power through. It took a long, long time to adjust. My body hurt all over. When I woke up every morning, I couldn't even walk properly. I had to hobble around like I had arthritis in my legs and feet, and usually by the time I left the house for work, my feet were still pretty sore. It wasn't all bad though. I liked my new team, my new team leader was a pretty good guy and easy to work with. I picked up the jobs they gave me pretty easily, but there was one thing that kept eating me up.

Every month that went by, it seemed like I wasn't any closer to getting full time. I started to really lose it at this point. I had a tooth slowly rotting away on me. I had to wash my mouth out with liquor every morning and every night just to numb the pain. I couldn't afford a dentist, I couldn't get to a dental college for a freebie pull or fillings. I just had to deal. Eventually the pain just became part of the background noise: another bit of misery to add to the weight. All in all, though, I was doing ok.

Then I got moved again. Not to another part of the plant, just another team in the same area. I didn't want to be moved, I had heard enough about the other team leader to know I wasn't going to enjoy being under his command, but I didn't get a say in it. They shoved me onto his team, and that? That was when the place really became Hell on Earth for me. See, this guy was just about the worst boomer stereotype you could imagine. He'd been with the plant since it'd opened its doors thirty years ago, and apparently felt that, despite the fact he had never risen higher than a Team Leader position (the lowest rung on the management ladder), he was the sole authority on 'How Things Were'. To make it worse, he'd decided I was a piece of shit before I was even moved to his team. We'd had an encounter previously where he tried to give me an order, and since he wasn't my superior at the time I didn't answer to him, I told him no.

He was (and still is) also a bitter, spiteful, petty hypocrite with a cruel streak a mile long. When they introduced a new model of car, he spent most of the shift completely up my ass, constantly hassling me about not working fast enough. His chosen favorites could do whatever they wanted, fuck up whenever they wanted, got all the best jobs, but me and the other 'undesirables'? No such mercy for us. I worked myself to the point of heat exhaustion in my first summer under him, just trying to meet the crotchety old fucker's standards. More than once he pushed me to the verge of cussing him out like the miserable sack of shit he was. The boomer always had an opinion about everyone and everything. I have seen him verbally and emotionally abuse multiple employees in the two years since I joined his team, I can't even keep track of how many people he's run off. You may be asking yourself how he can get away with such behavior, well it's really quite simple: He's fucking ancient. He could literally retire any day but he doesn't because it would mean forfeiting the last little mote of power the petty would-be Tyrant has. The company won't touch him. I'm pretty sure nothing short of actual physical assault on his part would make them take action.

So, I was usually walking about twenty miles a day to get two and from work. When I could find a ride, I took it. Some of my fellow employees got sick of picking me up off the side of the road and flat out demanded that I start riding in and out with them, which made things a lot easier. Words cannot express how grateful I was to those people. If you've never had to spend two or three hours marching in sweltering heat, pouring rain, or freezing cold, let me tell you: It's an experience you can happily skip. My first two winters at the plant, my hands got so dried out the skin around my knuckles and between my fingers cracked, flaked, and sometimes even turned purple. Just doing my job was all kinds of agony. On top of that, I was constantly being harassed and hounded by the Boomer and his Minions. Worse though? Watching the months crawl by while being told over and over and over again that I was just one moment away from making it: transcending Temp Status and finally, FINALLY achieving the coveted title of 'Associate'.

All in all, it took two and a half years. In terms of attendance and performance, I was a model employee for the company. I never went into their disciplinary program, I was never late, I did my job so well that even my shitbag Team Leader started struggling to find reasons to fuck me over. I argued and clashed with my Team Leader a lot, but just as they wouldn't touch him, the company also didn't come after me, since I had plenty of people keeping an eye on my Team Leader. They knew what he was like, how he operated. The guys on my old team especially, they always went to bat for me, even when I didn't ask them to. Hell, they did it even when I specifically begged them not to. The cynic in me says they were just hoping I'd be what got the old bastard fired, but there's a small part of me that does believe, deep down, they really were just trying to look out for me. I hated it so much, being so helpless. It was like being in high school again, having to just take all that fucking abuse and do nothing to retaliate. Some days when he went off, it was all I could do to keep from breaking his jaw. I'd never wished violence on the elderly before I met this asshole, but now? It's an almost daily occurrence.

As far as my Team Leader was concerned, 'the lazy, entitled young white men' were ruining the company. In his eyes, we were worthless (except for his favorites). Women, People of Color? They got a pass from him. The old fucker's whiter and a thousand times more entitled than me or anyone else on the team, and every god damn one of us works together, as a unit. No one was happy about his 'White Guilt' ridden speeches or his lectures on how worthless and two-timing unions were. Honestly, he swings so hard from the Right end of the Spectrum to the Left and back again that it's damn near impossible to be certain what he's gonna say and when he's gonna say it. You can damn well be certain, however, that it will always be a lecture, he will always find someone to belittle and bully, and everyone will be made uncomfortable by what he has to say.

My tooth eventually abscessed, but with how much we were working at the time, it was just impossible to find a dentist who could get the job done. I had insurance now that I was full time, proper insurance that is, but by then it was too late. The pain was unbelievable: it was like someone was sticking an electrified ice pick into my gums. I wasn't sleeping, I was constantly tired and miserable, stressed to the extreme and all kinds of furious at everything and everyone. I keep saying it, because it's true, but I was not in my right mind towards the end there.

One night, the line didn't stop for our scheduled break, costing me a minute. I know that doesn't sound like much, but I'm a smoker, and it's a two or three minute walk to the nearest smoke shack outside the building. So one minute stolen from my break is one minute less I spend resting and recouping, less time to smoke my damn cigarette and get a bit of space. I fucking lost it. I was cussing all the way back to the line, and my TL took that as an invitation to tell me all about how my attitude was a problem. He got in my face, about an inch away from me, shouting at the top of his lungs. I remember glancing at a tool nearby and thinking about how badly I wanted to smash his head in with it.

Luckily, before I really lost my control, my TL's direct superior showed up on the scene and de-escalated things. I had about a minute to myself, realized just how close I'd come to crossing a line, and pretty much shut down for the rest of the night. I finally got the tooth pulled a few weeks later. Antibiotics had killed the infection, so it wasn't as bad as it had been, but the subtler symptoms of intense dental pain remained. When I finally, finally got that tooth pulled? When the pain finally stopped? Mother of God, it was like I had suddenly sobered up after being shitfaced drunk. I could think clearly, I was calm, I was...well, normal, I guess.

That was a little more than a year ago. Since then we've come to something of a Cease-Fire. I don't mess with him, he doesn't mess with me. A lot has changed now, I guess. I had been running like crazy for so long, I let go of everything that I thought was weighing me down. I had to let go of everything just to keep moving forward. In the time since I joined up with the plant, I'd learned a lot more about their offered college programs...they were basically useless outside the factory. I could probably take them to another factory, sure, but none of them were anything even remotely approaching a way out of that fucking place. Realizing that even if I took their courses, I'd still be stuck at the plant was the final nail in the coffin for my dreams.

Now, here I am. Mercifully, my TL is FINALLY retiring this year. I'll be free of him, thank God, and I honestly cannot imagine that whoever replaces the bastard will be worse than he was. Just as bad? Sure, it could happen, but worse? No. I'll fucking dance when that bastard is gone.

There's no joy in this life, not for me at any rate. The factory has consumed me. Sometimes I still have fleeting fantasies of living in a little house in the middle of nowhere.

I always wanted to be a writer, to tell stories, but I've let go of that dream too. I don't have dreams any more. I just have the work. There's no room for them, there's no room for anything. I'm practically married to my job, and as much as I despise it, what am I gonna do? Quit? No one around here is going to hire a two time college drop out with no marketable skills and little experience in anything but the kind of work an inbred chimp could do, not for the kind of money I make at this plant. I can't afford to move to a different state, never mind another country. I fell in a big god damned concrete hole and now I'm just stuck there. Still waiting to die.

Since the pandemic, the big story has been about the rising inflation and the cost-of-living crisis impacting nearly everyone throughout the country. But the reality is that the cost of goods and services has been increasing for quite some time.

The Theft of a Decade tells about the state of people buying homes. "On the contrary, the rate of homeownership for young adults now is lower than in previous generations, even among those who have at least some college education. This is particular shock among people of color, for whom college was billed as an important boost into the middle class."

The rising cost of housing is partly because we aren't building enough housing, but we aren't building affordable starter homes that get people onto the property ladder. Sternberg says again, "Between 2012 and 2018, starter homes on the market declined both in absolute numbers (about half as many are available for purchase now as were available six years ago) and as a proportion of overall inventory (22 percent of homes for sale in the first quarter of 2018 were starter homes, compared to 30 percent in 2012)." After looking at several charts and a great deal of data, he goes on to state, "New house construction as a percentage of the total number of households in

America is the lowest it has been since data began in 1957." Sternberg laments, "Millennials have little choice but to hang on in our rented homes until we can afford the bigger, newer, more polished homes that are on the market."

THE GREAT FINANCIAL CRISIS AND HOUSING

The 2008 financial crisis changed America's housing market permanently. The reality is that the housing market has been distorted due to the securitization of mortgage debt coming out of the savings and loan crisis of the late 1980s, because of the implicit guarantee of mortgage companies Fannie Mae and Freddie Mac. Mortgages had become expensive debt assets, and junk debt spread throughout the system. A 1992 law set quotas for Fannie and Freddie to buy mortgages extended to low- and middle-income homebuyers even if those loans didn't otherwise satisfy Fannie's and Freddie's criteria.

In the name of encouraging homeownership, many buyers were issued loans for which they paid only interest for the first few years, in addition to not requiring any money down to establish equity in the house. Unless house values continued to rise rapidly and permanently, it would be years before this new cohort of homeowners truly owned anything. And that was one enormous "if." No one anticipated that the price of housing would ever fall. Then, one day, the price did fall. The prices of mortgage-backed securities plummeted as investors woke up to this new risk, blowing holes in bank balance sheets worldwide as the banks realized the assets they held, backed by risky mortgages, were worth less than they thought. The rest would be a particularly wretched bit of financial history. Unemployed homeowners started defaulting on their balloon payments when a crash in property values wiped out the equity mortgage lenders would ordinarily have recouped in foreclosures.

The contagion spread quickly throughout the financial system as mortgages went under, and the securities they backed also lost value. The problem was so significant that even a modest decrease in values sent portfolios plunging. Mortgage giants Fannie Mae and Freddie Mac were put into receivership, a form of bankruptcy. And then there was Lehman Brothers, the venerable investment bank that couldn't be rescued. Markets that had barely maintained their composure for a year and a half went into meltdown when Lehman tipped into bankruptcy in September 2008, with stock prices plunging around the globe.

In the days after the Lehman bankruptcy, credit markets froze. The massive insurance carrier AIG was on the hook for the insurance on these securities, and the value of the payouts was greater than the entire market capitalization of the venerable insurance giant. The Federal Reserve and the U.S. Treasury spent trillions to solve the problem. Between the $700 billion for TARP (temporary asset relief), $80 billion for AIG, and then bailouts for automakers and airlines, the bill for this financial crisis crossed into trillions. That doesn't include various loans to other banks and the recapitalization of European banks with U.S. dollars due to the debt crisis in Europe, which nearly collapsed the entire nation of Greece.

Rather than save regular people, the world's governments saved capital and assets. As Sternberg notes, "…keeping as many Boomers and Gen Xers as possible in homes they could barely afford while propping up prices so that Millennials would never be able to afford a house. In the depth of the crisis, lending for both new purchases and refinancing plunged, but after the crisis, only refinancing recovered significantly. But this artificial boost to prices has pushed the old-fashioned 20-percent-down, thirty-year amortizing, equity-accumulation-machine mortgages out of reach for millennials. We'll never be able to save that kind of down payment, so we don't. In 2017, the median down payment for a first-time buyer younger than thirty-seven was all of seven percent, and Fannie and the FHA still encourage first time buying with down payments as low as three percent."

If Timothy Geithner, Chairman of the Federal Reserve Bank of New York (and future treasury secretary) or Hank Paulson, U.S. Treasury Secretary, were thinking about the Japanese crisis of 1991, they didn't act like it. Much like their Japanese counterparts, their focus was to save the banking institutions. As Aaron Ross Sorkin has said in various videos and interviews on the 2008 crisis, "no one understood how close we came to ATMs not working."

COST OF HOUSING

It is no secret that millennials have struggled with the cost of housing and its rise in most locations. In no state in the U.S. can someone working minimum wage afford basic shelter. The situation is bleaker if that person has children. This has led to more people having roommates for longer and a steep rise in the multi-generational home. It is now a common march for younger people to bunk up with their parents. During the pandemic, both Gen Z and millennials (all well into their 30s) piled in with Mom and Dad. I also bunked with my parents for a few months during the pandemic after a break-up when I struggled to find a place to land. I was able to move out again and live on my own, but some are still stuck figuring things out in a market where the cost of housing increases yearly. Even with the wage premium brought on by the pandemic, a simple apartment in most of the country starts at $1,500. To find something lower, you'll have to look to more rural areas where jobs may be scarce.

The price of housing has affected millennial home buying. Fifty-two percent of millennials now own a home, impressive but still lagging behind previous generations. Even Gen Z has a higher home-ownership rate than millennials at the same age (according to Redfin). The cost of the great financial crisis continues to pile on. Millennials will never get those earning years back and the money and wealth generated from them. The cost of housing will leave some people behind forever, never to catch up to their peers, much less their parents.

BASEMENT DWELLINGS

It is a common trope to talk about people who live in their parent's basement, do everything online, and are essentially forever teenagers into their 30s. Much like the phenomena of NEETs that were discussed earlier, young people being stuck in a sort of purgatory is not always the explicit fault of the person in question. It is a symbol of a lack of opportunity. It can be a mental health problem, certainly, but too often, it is the result of economics. Moving out is expensive, and if the person has only worked service jobs, not gone to college or trade school, then they have probably bounced around from service job to service job, not making very much money and never being able to move on with their life. Eventually, they start doing other things for money, but now they are older, their resume is a patchwork quilt of various jobs, and no career path has emerged. It seems like too much of a bother to get another low-paying, low-dignity, low-prestige job where you work part-time or even full-time and simply can't support yourself as an independent adult. For those with the option to move back in with their parents or who never left, this can become a rather sad cycle of depression. Parents look at their children and wonder what went wrong. Much like the harried Japanese mothers wondering where they went wrong with their *hikikomori*, these parents wonder what is wrong and where they went wrong with parenting.

Another trend that has come out of the 2008 financial crisis is the rise of the multi-generation home. Stories abound of families who decide to build or buy large houses so that many generations can live under one roof. The advantages are on the cost side, especially for the younger folks. However, there are advantages, like having grandparents available for childcare and for grandparents to have help during a health crisis. There are worse outcomes for those who don't have the option of moving home or in with family.

Sternberg offers us this data about the problem. "As of 2014, living with parents was the most common living arrangement for young adults ages eighteen to thirty-four—for the first time in a hundred thirty years. Around 32 percent of people in that age bracket have moved back home or never left, compared to 31.6 percent who are living in their household with a partner or spouse. The other third lives with roommates, grandparents, or in a college dorm or prison." I should note that since the pandemic, this number has increased. The pandemic forced many young people back home or kept them there. Even millennials in their 30s were bunking up with their parents during the pandemic.

The cost of housing is such that working folks can end up with roommates in their 30s and early 40s. This is all about dollars and cents. The cost of housing is such that to make ends meet, a roommate may be required to secure housing. Either party is likely to be one paycheck away from ruination. In 2018, a much-ballyhooed survey of Americans stated that most of the country could not meet a $400 expense because they did not have $400 in savings. Having roommates isn't bad, but it is very different from having your place independently. It is no wonder that household formation is down and fewer people are having children.

SECTION 5:

IS THERE ANY HOPE?

Throughout this book, we've learned about the plight of America's lost generation from various angles, including the guidance we get from our friends in Japan. Now, there is only one question: Is there any hope? I started this book before the pandemic and worked on it during the long days of quarantine. The pandemic was a significant setback for millennials, much like the Asian Financial Crisis for Japanese people in 1997. In this section, we think about the future and how millennials might be able to improve their given lot in life.

CHAPTER 24:

CAN MILLENNIALS SAVE THEMSELVES?

I spoke with David Burstein, one of the people who had written about the trend with millennials early on. I noticed that in our conversation two stories emerged: the working-class story and the middle-class millennial story. He didn't seem to grasp the problems with working-class millennials as he focused primarily on millennials, who he described as performing "aspirational purchasing." These sorts of purchases track how Japanese young people acted after 1991 and often how they act to this day by buying luxury goods from popular European brands. He described most of millennials' financial issues as having to do with this aspirational purchasing. That idea certainly does not reflect the lived experience of the working- and middle-class millennials, but I will address this topic anyway.

Now, why is there aspirational purchasing? Because even for millennials who make decent money, the rewards they might have earned simply don't exist today. When you can't buy a house or afford childcare, coffee and avocado toast suddenly don't seem so bad.

For millennials who have made decent money, spending controls can help build savings. Given the cost of housing, the rising prices of homes, and the rising costs in a post-pandemic environment, even for middle- and upper-middle-class millennials, moving forward financially presents challenges. At least they have some resources to work with. Working-class millennials are plagued by stagnant wages that have only begun to improve after the pandemic and the Great Resignation.

Burstein's solution for millennials? He advised that we need to create a new meaning and fulfillment in life that doesn't include owning a home or having kids. This struck me as a bit odd. Most people want to reproduce and continue their family. It's a perfectly natural desire. As for owning a home, this is a uniquely American obsession that our European counterparts don't focus on as much, primarily due to the cost of housing and land in Europe. I think it might be a hard sell to millennials to say that the solution to having a fulfilling life is to rent forever, not have kids, and possibly not marry, even though married people make more money, are generally happier, and live longer. This is not how I would describe millennials as saving themselves.

To make life better for millennials, a series of policy changes must take place. We've already discussed some of them in this book, but the prescription for Americans is relatively simple: Prioritize people over asset prices. Asset prices have been artificially propped up, making housing far too expensive for most people to afford, leaving folks renting at ever higher prices. The cost of living needs to be controlled, and correspondingly wages need to grow meaningfully so that people can afford a decent living.

In the years after World War II, the country faced many problems similar to those it is now facing. While many compare the economy to the late 1970s, the late 1940s are a far better guide. America had a terrible cost of living crisis, a housing shortage, and rapid inflation from overspending during the war. We solved those problems by rebuilding Europe and Japan and building the suburbs, which expanded homeownership to Americans (primarily Caucasians—minorities were left out). We can find ways to fix these problems again. While we don't have a world to rebuild from scratch, we can build more housing and housing types. We can ensure we aren't artificially inflating asset prices with policy changes at the Federal Reserve. Without a concerted effort to make changes, the situation for millennials as they get older will continue to be bleak, much like what is happening now in Japan. The people left behind in 1991 have no stable employment or retirement, straining their national pension program. It is probably worth noting that Social Security will run out of money in 2035, long before millennials are ready to retire (more on that retirement bomb later).

Bolstering these social safety nets (like we did during the pandemic) is going to be the only answer, and the only way to pay for that will be to tax the wealthiest Americans and corporations. President Biden has made some intimations toward this goal. Still, his Build Back Better legislation stalled in Congress in 2021, and much of the American social safety net remains absent from our lives. Americans pay plenty in taxes at the city, county, state, and federal levels, and we get comparatively little for what we pay in taxes. This is another aspect of our society that needs to change if our lives are to improve. Without these changes, the future of millennials will remain bleak.

This is where the Japanese story comes full circle. The Japanese never solved their economic problems. It took a global pandemic to give them the inflation they craved for twenty-five years. The people left behind in the 1990s never really recovered. It's such a problem that their retirement system is struggling to cope. The lost decades of the Japanese economy have left nearly two generations of people behind now. For those who managed to graduate at the right time, get the right job, and function in society, it has been better than those for whom society simply left behind. However, even now, young Japanese are beginning to reject the punishing work culture and seek more independent ways of making money. The famous English-speaking YouTuber SoraTrolls spoke about this at length and how things are ever-so-slowly changing in Japan. If we look to our Japanese cousins for solutions to what millennials have been living through and what

Gen Z faces, they cannot offer us any hope beyond a sympathetic ear and a cup of tea. The Japanese government has hardly lifted a finger to help those left behind in the economic devastation of the 1990s. Now, as those people reach late middle age and retirement, the government is only now beginning to act. It is quite likely that millennials won't begin to solve their own problems until they get enough levers of power to make the changes necessary. Given how long the boomers have been in power and how Gen X folded like a deck of cards, it may be too late for many millennials.

FUTURE NOSTALGIA

Among many people in their 30s and early 40s is a longing for the future that we were deprived of due to decisions far beyond our control. Is it possible to be nostalgic for something that never existed? Indeed, many Trump supporters—including his millennial supporters, who tend to skew male—dream of an imaginary past of the United States that only existed for a select few, if it ever existed at all. For millennials, even the most liberal ones, the dream of a world where housing is affordable, wages outpace inflation, and the means of a decent living are well within reach for the majority of people remains an irresistible fantasy. In our modern age, it is not simply enough to have a job—one must have a job that pays enough for that decent living. Many people under 45 are not afforded that privilege in the wealthiest country on earth.

It is no shock that our culture looks to the past for inspiration. The world seemed simpler and more straightforward then. It had plenty of complications, but the lens of time tends to wash them away in favor of the good parts we remember. Meanwhile, the future is bleak for millennials on a variety of fronts. Climate change and shifting ecology will redefine how and where we live in our country. The declining living standards include failing infrastructure, natural disasters, and other problems that will strain systems.

The pandemic has already shown us empty grocery shelves and toilet paper becoming scarce. Years have passed, and this is still a reality in some places. Supply chain issues continue to disrupt the flow of goods and services. Instead of the stable global order that has existed since 1945, the geopolitical order is also in upheaval, and it seems like our world is beset with problems both within and without. It is not just income inequality, but how we live seems strained. There is little that works, and many people can't find a way to get ahead. The system appears to purposely hold people down and block upward mobility, which had become a hallmark of American life.

The big trouble is that it didn't have to be that way. The Great Prosperity of the middle of the century promised people from all backgrounds (people of color much later) the possibility of making a decent living and having a decent life. That was the actual achievement of the New Deal. Millennials were raised in a world that still believed that was possible; no one realized that the regulatory underpinnings that made that possible had undone that dream for all but a privileged few—much of what boomers and others hear as millennial whining is the grief of a future denied.

CHAPTER 25:

DEBT AND RETIREMENT

A submission from Reddit:

30M. I did get stuck working at Starbucks for six years.

I always envy big middle-class American families when I see them. They are so lucky to have all that loving family support, branching connections and big homes with dogs. They always have someone to talk to. It brings a tear to my eye when I see big family reunions and weddings. I have never experienced any of that because I live in poverty with my mom, brother and sister.

We're European immigrants. We moved to America when I was 12. My parents worked shitty jobs and eventually we got a tiny house which we still live in now. One tiny bathroom, thin walls, no basement and two bedrooms, Five People. Nevertheless, we managed to live in it, going on 15 years now. My dad slept on a couch in the living room. He passed away last year. Now there's four of us.

We were full of optimism a decade ago. I was in college. My dad was buying old cars and my brother was learning how to fix them up. I left college because I realized it was more of a business than an actual school. Often times I knew more than the professors. I'm glad I got out of there with only $20k in loans.

We're a well-read and practically intelligent family. We care for what little we own and we're grateful for it. My poor mother has been working her shitty housekeeping job in the ghetto for over 15 years now. I remember her coming home sometimes, telling me how badly Americans treat foreigners and she'll cry. It pissed me off so much. I knew that if I were ever in a good financial position, the very first thing I'd do is make sure my poor mum never had to work again and could actually enjoy what life she has left. Of course, that never happened.

I started working at Starbucks. That's when my slow death began. When they hired me I was an optimistic and energetic twenty-something. In retrospect, I now see how these corporations destroy our own young adults. These food and retail jobs are killing our own citizens! I developed depression and anxiety within a couple of years. It's a degrading and dehumanizing job and no matter how I tried to combat the effects, the wage slavery got the best of me. Over the years I watched countless young people get hired. They went from wide-eyed and optimistic to picking up smoking and sugar, and developing depression and sleeping issues in about a years' time. All of them. The company throws them out and hires fresh "bodies." That's what management refers to us quite frequently, "bodies." By dehumanizing the workforce, it makes it easy for management to treat us like mere numbers. The company has nothing to worry about because, thanks to social media, young people falsely assume that working at Starbucks is a cool and hipster experience.

So there are always fresh, energetic bodies applying for Starbucks. And corporate loves fresh bodies.

I noticed that my entire family developed depression. My mom, bless her heart, is the only one still trying so hard every day to be positive. My brother completely stopped talking, he just stays in his room or fixes things. My brother is a genius who taught himself how to code, and he trades stocks and rebuilds car engines; yet he's so alone, so poor, just sits in his room and it breaks my fucking heart. My sister probably has developed the worst depression. She doesn't talk either, just goes to her shitty job and comes home. I'm the eldest and it's a daily battle for me. I'm extremely frugal; we all are. I prefer to be left alone most of the time. I like to go running on trail and reading psychology, philosophy, and neuroscience, and learning about physics and evolutionary biology. It's a battle to hold myself together. I see no path forward at all. I have lost all energy and desire to get some career. I'm thirty now and still living in that tiny home. We have no friends and zero connections. The only way to live now is to be a good stoic. To learn to accept things how they are. I cannot tell you how depressing it is to be a 30 year old adult still living at home with mom. It stunts growth. I wonder how many people out there are stuck just like me.

It's easy for others to suggest to just "get a career" or "be an electrician." When someone has been broken for years and lost all hope and developed mental issues, that person is not interested in anything anymore. That person only feels worse when others tell them to "pull themselves up by their bootstraps" and do this or that.

The tragedy, in my mind, is that we are such a humble and kind family and yet we got fucking stuck in this mud.

It doesn't seem fair at all. We are such nice and mindful people. We deserve to live in a larger home, in a better location instead of this ghetto. Maybe near some trees and two bathrooms at very least. It would be a dream come true for us. It's not fucking fair! I don't know what's next. I contemplated quitting and just being homeless. Throw on a backpack and hike all the way to California or something. I've never been outside of rural Illinois, we could never afford to travel or vacation. I've only seen mountains in pictures.

I often times spend hours browsing decent homes for sale on Zillow and daydreaming about what it would be like to live there. I imagine being happy, finding like-minded friends, maybe even starting a family, diving into hobbies, and enjoying nice roads in a sports car. These are dreams that I know will never happen. It's already too late. I stopped believing in free-will. This life is just a lottery. If you're born in the right place, right time, and by random chance you encounter the right people and the right circumstances, then you become a reflection of that. Hard work comes naturally to people to whom the environment fosters quick feedback and reward. You are a reflection of your environment.

Poverty inside a country is like an ant colony with immobilized ants. In order to make decisions and move in life, you need money. It really bothers me to no end that we don't want our own country to improve. How fucking embarrassing it is that our advanced civilization in 2020 still accepts having poverty. It's like, we don't want to progress forward. To become the best we can be as quickly as possible.

Humans are the life-blood of a country. If individuals within a system cannot afford to freely move about and make decisions, then the system as a whole suffers.

RETIREMENT

After WWII, GIs came home to a very different labor market. The gains of the labor movement during the Depression had become common practice. Large companies boasted defined benefit pension plans, on-site doctors, and high unionization rates. The eight-hour workday and the weekend off had become mostly standard. Social Security kept older adults alive. Government-funded unemployment insurance helped workers transition between jobs.

The lives of these men (women were often let go when the war was over) would be better than their fathers' were. They would enjoy good jobs, decent wages, upward mobility, and the benefits of those gains. Retirement, the point at which people could leave the workforce, was now an option for the working classes. It was the luxury of freedom in one's twilight years. Focusing on this would become an essential part of American and European society. The ability to stop working and continue living at a decent standard of living had been impossible for the regular working-class person before World War II.

With wages rising, productivity rising, and most people having access to social benefits through their employer, an imperfect but somewhat stable system persisted.

However, this all began to change in the late 1970s and early 1980s. The defined pension benefit was out, and the 401k was in. In *The Theft of a Decade*, we find out that "A long-term trend in American retirement planning has been the shift out of old-fashioned defined-benefit pension plans (where the employer saves and invests a large pot of money on behalf of its employees and then pays a guaranteed annual amount in retirement) and into defined-contribution plans such as a 401(k), where the employer pays a set percentage of salary into a tax-free investment account each year, which the worker can use in retirement.... But pardon millennials if we don't laugh—because to an astounding degree, we all are our parents' retirement plans."

The reality is that millennials not making enough money and not participating in the labor force has a deleterious effect on the entire pension and Social Security system, which millennials are responsible for keeping going. According to the Congressional Budget Office, Social Security will run out of money to pay out benefits in 2035. Sternberg writes about this crisis. "The one thing that unites all these fiscal gaps, whether for Social Security, Medicare, or state and local pensions, is that someone will have to pay more for them in the future, or some beneficiaries will have to receive less. That means everyone— and especially Boomers— should be frightened that since 2008, the main entitlement trend has been that Millennials are losing the ability to pay for these benefits. The evaporation of a political willingness to pay won't be far behind."

He says about the fiscal gap that "Today's taxpayers, which increasingly means Millennials, in fact, are already paying. In 2017, the interest that Treasury paid to Social Security on the bonds in the trust fund—interest paid out of general tax revenues—accounted for $83.2 billion in revenue just for the old-age portion of the program excluding disability insurance, helping to fill what otherwise would have been a $64 billion gap between tax receipts and benefits paid."

It's not just their parents and grandparents' retirement that millennials aren't funding. They can't afford to fund their own retirements either. Sternberg writes again, "Another study based on a regularly conducted government survey found that a depressing 66 percent of working Millennials had nothing saved for retirement and not for lack of trying; although most of them worked for employers who offered retirement plans to some workers, 40 percent of Millennials weren't eligible to participate because they didn't work enough hours or didn't have enough tenure under their belts."

A recent opinion piece in *The New York Times* announced that as millennials hit middle age, it's not looking like what we were promised. A Twitter/X commentator, who shall remain unmentioned, said, "Nobody promised you spoiled brats anything." That is the attitude towards millennials in a tweet. Even in middle age, as boomers were ascendant and were changing American culture in their own image at every level, millennials are reaching the same stage and finding that middle age is not what we expected or hoped to experience. The only reply is more of the same "entitled" attitude that older people have always had toward millennials.

DEBT

College debt was mostly unheard of for the middle-century working class because many colleges were free or inexpensive. Consumer debt was nominal and was mostly for cars and housing. Credit card debt had yet to raise its ugly head in the lives of the average American. Most Americans only owed money on their houses and sometimes their cars.

In the 1980s, this began to change with the rise of consumer credit cards. Companies like Visa, Mastercard, American Express, and others began to issue cards that people could use anywhere. Society moved away from an all-cash consumption system to a debt-based system. Flashy ads with beautiful people using their "BankAmericard" and other such clever names for these new cards seemed to offer consumers a new way to spend and maintain their lifestyles. In an unattributed video, a "person on the street" interview was done in the late 1990s asking people how much credit card debt they owed. People casually reported that they owed $10,000 or much more but didn't seem worried about it and kept smiling and looking happy.

Debt consumption fueled much of the growth in the 1990s. Debt-relief services crept in to help people deal with all the debt that they had taken on. In 2008, this system of debt fell apart spectacularly. Debt collapse is not a new economic phenomenon either. The Normans had a debt collapse in the thirteenth century when the trade of debt owed by landowners grew greater than the income from the debts. Kept track of on elaborate sticks with strings, this was one of the first debt bubbles, and when it burst, it collapsed the Norman economy for decades.

Debt accrues across credit cards and car loans. For most Americans, having a car is not an optional feature of life—it is essential. Car loans have gotten longer over the past decade. Some financing companies are offering loans for up to seven years. Car payments are also increasing along with the terms of the loans, and the price of a new car has climbed ever higher too. The popularity of credit services that allow you to pay for the purchase over time is symbolic of how debt is part and parcel of American life. It can be easy for the debt to become overwhelming, yet it seems essential to life due to the increased cost of living.

On the website "Desdemona Despair" in 2019, they wrote about new polling data that showed both Gen X and millennials are stressed about debt and finances. "Millennials are known for being financially behind thanks to the fallout of the Great Recession, high costs of living, and staggering student-loan debt—but Gen X is just as nearly stressed about money, especially when it comes to debt. Of the respondents who answered, more than half of all millennials and Gen X respondents said that they were stressed "some" or "a lot" about their credit card, personal loan, or student loan debts."

The student loan crisis is the outsized example of how millennials and some of their Gen X cousins have been burdened with the cost of higher education. For millennials, and to an even greater degree Gen X, debt has been something that has chased them their entire adult lives. The reality is that student loan debt is only a problem for a minority of millennials who went (or tried) to go to college. For the last fifteen years, this has been one of the most prominent talking points for millennials, and it was only in 2020 that it finally became a national electoral issue. President Biden ran on student loan forgiveness, and although his first plan would eventually be struck down by the Supreme Court in 2023, the student loan crisis will still be a front-and-center issue in American politics.

DEATHS OF DESPAIR

In 2017, *The Spokesman-Review,* the daily newspaper in Spokane, Washington, ran a story on the rise of substance abuse and deaths of despair among an increasingly younger cohort of people. The article begins with this haunting story, "Ryan Johnson was 22 when he succumbed to a heroin addiction that had intensified as the Erie, Pennsylvania, high school graduate grew disillusioned with his future. His mother found him in his room with his head slumped and lips blue. It was June 28, 2014, the day of his sister's master's degree graduation party. 'He just saw his life as not what he wanted it to be, and he didn't know how to get it there,' said Sue Johnson, who lay next to her son's corpse for an hour. He had dropped out of a two-year culinary program and was working part-time, low-wage jobs. He often compared himself with his peers in college and his athletic, academic older sister."

The remainder of the article lists all the complaints we know in the millennial story. Marriage happens later, religious affiliation is down, and, of course, the tough job market all piles into a perfect storm whose products are the pipe and needle. According to the same article, "Nationally, 25- to 34-year-olds make up the biggest share of opioid overdoses, and their proportion has been climbing, based on Kaiser Family Foundation data. 'It stems from depression,' said Jack Martin, a 63-year-old funeral director who's dealt with many overdose deaths. That's especially true for younger victims. 'When they look down the road: Am I going to get married? Am I going to be successful? Am I going to have enough money?'"

In the medical profession, it is difficult to treat people whose only actual treatment can come from a change in their material circumstances. Doctors loving refer to it as "shit life disease." The meaning is clear, the only thing wrong with the person is that their life is shit, and the only real treatment would be the resources to solve their real problems. The blog Desdemona Despair reposted a June 2019 *Time* magazine article by Jamie Ducharme that said, "More millennials are also dying 'deaths of despair,' or deaths related to drugs, alcohol, and suicide." The article cited a report by the public-health groups Trust for America's Health and Well Being Trust. While these deaths have increased across all ages in the past ten years, they've increased the most among younger Americans, Ducharme said. They accounted for the deaths of about 36,000 American millennials in 2017 alone, according to the report. Drug overdoses were the most common cause of death.

According to the CDC, from 2007 to 2017, adults ages 18 to 34 saw a 69 percent increase in alcohol-related deaths, a 108 percent increase in drug-related deaths—fueled mainly by the opioid crisis—and a 35 percent increase in deaths by suicide. Most of the deaths had to do with overdoses from the opioid crisis, but other drugs contributed as well, and the 35 percent increase in suicide is probably the most troubling figure from that data. A death of despair occurs when someone's life is so broken and so troubled that they see no other escape and no other option but to commit suicide. Sometimes, it is the intention, and sometimes, it is simply death by attrition due to addiction. Doctors have even coined the phrase "shit life syndrome." The physical health of this generation has been hurt by how the modern economic and social system has robbed them of the promise and hope that seemed to be a birthright.

Millennials have come to accept many things about their futures. The possibility of buying a home is simply not possible for many. Some can't afford to have children or have decided not to for social reasons. This leaves many people feeling adrift, as stated in a 2020 article in *Maclean's* magazine in Canada. The article was titled "Directionless and Lost: What it means to be a millennial, for a reason." When you have a persistent crisis in society, not everyone will survive. The trouble is that this was already a problem heading into the pandemic, and then the pandemic made the trend far worse. Mental health has gone from a buzzword to a national debate. Between mass shootings and Jimmy

Carter-esque feelings of malaise, it should be no surprise that some people would choose to end their lives.

When online commenters or others remark that millennials are whining on unnecessarily, it is hard not to take a cynical view when the causes of those complaints are killing people. The pandemic has been a terrible blow to a generation already on its heels. The fact that it has persisted this long means that for many millennials, this is the end of the economic road. There will be little opportunity from here on out, and this comes just as millennials reach their peak earning years. It seems that given what we know about the opioid crisis and these deaths of despair, solving these problems should be a priority for the government, yet it isn't.

CHAPTER 26:

CONCLUSIONS

"The Millennials entered the workforce during the worst downturn since the Great Depression. Saddled with debt, unable to accumulate wealth, and stuck in low-benefit, dead-end jobs, they never gained the financial security their parents, grandparents, or even older siblings enjoyed. They are now entering their peak earning years in the midst of an economic cataclysm more severe than the Great Recession, near guaranteeing that they will be the first generation in modern American history to end up poorer than their parents. Compounding their troubles, Millennials are, for now, disproportionate holders of the kind of positions disappearing the fastest: bartenders, half of restaurant workers, and a large share of retail workers. For the most part, kids of the 1980s and 1990s did it right: They avoided drugs and alcohol as adolescents. They went to college in record numbers. They sought stable, meaningful jobs and stable, meaningful careers. A lot of good that did."

—Annie Lowry, 2022

You'll have noticed that I've returned to a quote I presented in Chapter 2. It provides important context. We've seen all the different ways in which millennials—now reaching middle age—and their Gen Z cousins (to a similar but lesser degree) have become lost. After digesting all this information, it is helpful to pull back and see the big picture of what most people under 50 have faced. We've lost the engine of common prosperity that worked well for the boomers. I would say that is the over-arching message of this book.

The situation for millennials is rather bleak. Between the Great Recession, the pandemic, and the economic upheavals that those events caused, alongside globalization and other massive economic changes, millennials have become the first members of America's precariat. The lower down the socioeconomic ladder you go, the worse it gets. One of the most prominent stories of this generation is the downward mobility of the children of the upper classes and the lack of upward mobility for those who aspired from the working class. It is a personally devastating thing to put in the work and take on the debt required to go to school to advance one's career prospects, only to find that it was unnecessary for the jobs that were available. Those who could take opportunities to work in unpaid internships or had connections to jobs have fared much better than those who were trying to be upwardly mobile and needed to make those networking connections. This dichotomy has spread on social media. I have observed it among many of my college friends, who seem to be vice presidents or similarly titled at Company XYZ. However, as we have learned from the heartfelt stories in this book, that experience is not widespread, and many other people have been left behind in an economy that does not work for the majority but rather for the wealth of a few.

Unfortunately, the comparison between Japan and the United States became more pronounced while writing this book. When I began writing this book in 2020, it was early in the pandemic, and the U.S. had terrible deflation and was facing uncertain economic times. When I finished this book in the fall of 2023, a low growth and stagflationary economy were well upon Americans. Inflation has skyrocketed the price of pretty much everything.

For millennials to change the end of this story to be different from Japan's will take political will that I don't yet see in the American electorate. Millennials can attack the neoliberal economic nature of the American economy. Like their forebears in the early twentieth century, they can attack the concentration of wealth at the top with new taxes. They can form companies owned by the workers rather than the owners of capital and their lackeys. Indeed, younger people look more favorably on socialism than their parents did. In a Pew Research survey, those under 40 viewed socialism positively. A great deal of this change is due to the internet. Americans have figured out that we aren't number one at everything and that other countries have brilliant ways of doing things. Universal healthcare is normal in every other industrialized nation except the United States. Generous maternity and paternity leave for parents and childcare is often standard too. These benefits are absent from the American way of life. For younger Americans, this is what socialism means. It means that the wealthy and the corporations pay their fair share to support a society that supports their great wealth.

I am also left with a few ideas still banging around in my head. One of them is from a Twitter/X thread from user 'Wayneburkett' I read a while back that stated, "The fact is that like 90% of Americans have healthcare, 65% of Americans live in owner-occupied housing (a number that's been stable for four decades), and only about 13% of Americans have student loans… One thing that can be hard to accept if you're struggling is that there are hundreds of millions of Americans who are doing just fine. People will see a new apt building and exclaim, 'nobody can afford that rent!' but what might depress you more is that lots of people can."

This quote has bothered me since I read it—not only because it is condescending and dismissive, but because he isn't entirely wrong about the situation. I saved it and have reread it multiple times. I wrote an entire book centered on the message that we are not alright—and that we are heading toward unfortunate outcomes as we lurch toward the kinds of economic and social conditions that have plagued Japan for the past thirty years.

This is balanced with Jim Rickards agreeing that we never recovered from the Great Recession and have been in a prolonged depression. I've written two articles on that very subject. However, perhaps the uncomfortable fact about this book is that it is a story about the aspirational working class, persons trying to stay middle class, and others on the margins. A large portion of the populace fits the narrative I quoted above. Most people are doing alright, but for those who struggle, it might seem like the economy is terrible and the United States is in decline. Indeed, seeing the tent cities in most major American cities doesn't inspire confidence in a booming American economy. But for many Americans, the economy is doing fine. I think that is likely why there is a social media obsession, especially among young men, chasing material wealth, just like young people in Japan chase luxury goods.

America is supposed to be a country of class mobility, but it hasn't been that way for some time. For those blessed with resources and young people blessed with family resources, it quite likely seems like the American system is working just fine. For those who are young, starting from nothing, are the first in their family to go to college, or are an immigrant, the promise of America has often not delivered. I do find it interesting that when I first posted on Reddit about this project and solicited the stories that are contained within these pages, people on r/lostgeneration came forth with a variety of experiences, including one young man of 22 who was working as a plumber and reported that his life had been fine. He was making great money, "just for another perspective," he remarked.

In writing this, I find myself speaking for those who have been disregarded, dismissed, and discarded by society. Those young people, now approaching middle age, are wondering where everything went wrong and are pessimistic about ever improving. There is no shortage of calls on social media to reform the system, end capitalism, or the perennial favorite, "eat the rich." I don't think they would taste good, but the point is that there are enough people who are unhappy with how the system works and how people are thrown aside. The question remains: Is there enough of them to generate real change? This is an area where I can't offer any solace. I saw how Occupy withered and how other movements have come and gone with little being changed. Indeed, it does seem like we are, in the words of British documentarian Adam Curtis, "watched over by the machines of loving grace."

BIBLIOGRAPHY

All interviews in this book were conducted through Reddit anonymously and their stories are included with full consent.

Association for Psychological Science. "How Poverty Affects the Brain and Behavior." *Association for Psychological Science*. Accessed May 26, 2025. https://www.psychologicalscience.org/news/releases/how-poverty-affects-the-brain-and-behavior.html.

Blanchflower, David G. *Not Working: Where Have All the Good Jobs Gone?* Princeton, NJ: Princeton University Press, 2019.

Brynjolfsson, Erik. "The Turing Trap: The Promise & Peril of Human-Like Artificial Intelligence." *Daedalus* 151, no. 2 (2022): 272–287. https://doi.org/10.1162/daed_a_01915.

Cowan, Cameron Lee. *What the Hell Is Going On?: A Primer to Understanding Our World in the Age of Trump.* 1st ed. Washington, D.C.: Widgery Omnimedia, 2019.

Cowley, Stacy. "Little of the Paycheck Protection Program's $800 Billion Protected Paychecks." *The New York Times*, February 1, 2022. https://www.nytimes.com/2022/02/01/business/ppp-loans-small-business.html.

Desdemona Despair. *Blogging the End of the World*™. https://desdemonadespair.net/.

Dolan, Eric W. "New Study Indicates That Potential Partners Experience a Large Penalty for Being Black on Dating Apps." *PsyPost*, July 18, 2021. https://www.psypost.org/new-study-indicates-that-potential-partners-experience-a-large-penalty-for-being-black-on-dating-apps/.

Ducharme, Jamie. "More Millennials Are Dying 'Deaths of Despair,' as Overdose and Suicide Rates Climb." *Time*, June 13, 2019. https://time.com/5606411/millennials-deaths-of-despair/.

Eberstadt, Nicholas. *Men Without Work: Post-Pandemic Edition.* 2nd ed. West Conshohocken, PA: Templeton Press, 2022.

Elliott, Alicia. "Directionless and Lost." *Maclean's*, Month Day, Year. https://www.macleans.ca/article-url. Accessed May 26, 2025.

Elliott, Alicia. "Directionless and Lost: What It Means to Be a Millennial." *Maclean's*, October 15, 2018. https://macleans.ca/society/life/directionless-and-lost-what-it-means-to-be-a-millennial/.

Franklin, H. Bruce. "Why Talk about Loans?" *CounterPunch*, August 31, 2022. https://www.counterpunch.org/2022/08/31/why-talk-about-loans/.

Gallup. "Democrats More Positive About Socialism Than Capitalism." *Gallup.com*, August 13, 2018. https://news.gallup.com/poll/240725/democrats-positive-socialism-capitalism.aspx.

Hanson, Victor Davis. "The Liberal Arts Weren't Murdered — They Committed Suicide." *National Review*, December 18, 2018. https://www.nationalreview.com/2018/12/liberal-arts-were-not-murdered-they-committed-suicide/.

Harris, Adam. "The Liberal Arts May Not Survive the 21st Century." *The Atlantic*, December 13, 2018. https://www.theatlantic.com/education/archive/2018/12/the-liberal-arts-may-not-survive-the-21st-century/577876/.

Hemingway, Ernest. *The Sun Also Rises*. New York: Charles Scribner's Sons, 1926.

Herbenick, Debby, Molly Rosenberg, Lilian Golzarri-Arroyo, J. Dennis Fortenberry, and Tsung-chieh Fu. "Changes in Penile-Vaginal Intercourse Frequency and Sexual Repertoire from 2009 to 2018: Findings from the National Survey of Sexual Health and Behavior." *Archives of Sexual Behavior* 51, no. 4 (2022): 1419–1433. https://doi.org/10.1007/s10508-021-02125-2.

Kaplan, Juliana. "Boomers Are Buying Up All the Homes, and Millennials Are Scrambling to Keep Up." *Business Insider*, April 17, 2023. https://www.businessinsider.com/boomers-buying-homes-zblocking-millennials-housing-market-real-estate-prices-2023-4.

Keles, Betul, Niall McCrae, and Annemarie Graeilst. "A Systematic Review: The Influence of Social Media on Depression, Anxiety and Psychological Distress in Adolescents." *International Journal of Adolescence and Youth* 25, no. 1 (2020): 79–93. https://doi.org/10.1080/02673843.2019.1590851.

Klein, Matthew C. "Let's Overshoot." *The Overshoot*, February 17, 2021. https://the-overshoot.co/p/lets-overshoot.

Kyodo News. "Japan's Disadvantaged Generation Seek Changes in Hiring Practices." *Kyodo News*, July 4, 2019. https://english.kyodonews.net/news/2019/07/8b-4b3a2b5555-focus-japans-disadvantaged-generation-seek-changes-in-hiring-practices.html.

Lowry, Annie [@AnnieLowry]. Twitter post, summer 2020. https://twitter.com/AnnieLowry.

McWilliams, James. "The Humanities Are Dead. Long Live the Humanities." *Pacific Standard*, August 10, 2017. https://psmag.com/education/the-humanities-are-dead-long-live-the-humanities.

Mobius, Markus M., and Tanya S. Rosenblat. "Why Beauty Matters." *American Economic Review* 96, no. 1 (2006): 222–235. https://doi.org/10.1257/000282806776157515.

Nikkei Asian Review. "Lost Generation Haunts Japan, Abe, and the BOJ." *Nikkei Asian Review*, 2018.

Nikkei Asian Review. "Nightmare 2040: Japan's Lost Generation." *Nikkei Asian Review*, 2019.

O'Connor, Kate. "Lost Generation." *Great Writers Inspire*, University of Oxford. https://www.greatwritersinspire.com/writers-and-their-work/lost-generation.

O'Neill, Rachel. "Online Dating Apps Are Actually Kind of a Disaster." *Wired*, May 18, 2021. https://www.wired.com/story/online-dating-apps-are-a-disaster/.

Parker, Laura. "Why Humanities Matter in a STEM World." *Pacific Standard*, May 10, 2018. https://psmag.com/education/why-humanities-matter-in-a-stem-world.

Pesek, William. *Japanization: What the World Can Learn from Japan's Lost Decades*. Singapore: Bloomberg Press, 2014.

Piketty, Thomas. *Capital in the Twenty-First Century*. Translated by Arthur Goldhammer. Cambridge, MA: Belknap Press of Harvard University Press, 2014.

PsyPost. "New Study Indicates That Potential Partners Experience a Large Penalty for Being Black on Dating Apps." *PsyPost*, July 18, 2021. https://www.psypost.org/new-study-indicates-that-potential-partners-experience-a-large-penalty-for-being-black-on-dating-apps/.

Reddit. "r/lostgeneration." https://www.reddit.com/r/lostgeneration/.

Silver, Nate. "What Is Driving Growth in Government Spending?" *FiveThirtyEight (blog)*, *The New York Times*, January 17, 2013. https://fivethirtyeight.com/features/what-is-driving-growth-in-government-spending/.

Smialek, Jeanna. "Deaths of Despair: Millennials Turn to Drugs, Suicide in Unforgiving Job Market." *The Spokesman-Review*, April 19, 2017. https://www.spokesman.com/stories/2017/apr/19/deaths-of-despair-stalk-millennials-in-unforgiving/.

Sternberg, Joseph C. *The Theft of a Decade: Baby Boomers, Millennials, and the Distortion of Our Economy*. 1st ed. New York: PublicAffairs, 2019.

Stillman, Jessica. "Stop Bashing Liberal Arts Degrees. This New Analysis Shows They're a Good Investment." *Inc.*, February 19, 2019. https://www.inc.com/jessica-stillman/new-economic-analysis-getting-a-liberal-arts-degree-is-totally-a-good-investment.html.

Stover, Justin. "There Is No Case for the Humanities." *American Affairs Journal*, November 2017. https://americanaffairsjournal.org/2017/11/no-case-humanities/.

The Motley Fool. "Are You Well-Paid? Compare Your Salary to the Average U.S. Income." *The Motley Fool*, May 20, 2024. https://www.fool.com/money/research/average-us-income/.

The New York Times

Thompson, Derek. "Why Are Millions of Prime-Age Men Missing From the Economy?" *The Atlantic*, June 27, 2016. https://www.theatlantic.com/business/archive/2016/06/the-missing-men/488858/.

Thompson, Derek. "Your Brain on Poverty: Why Poor People Seem to Make Bad Decisions." *The Atlantic*, November 22, 2013. https://www.theatlantic.com/business/archive/2013/11/your-brain-on-poverty-why-poor-people-seem-to-make-bad-decisions/281780/.

Tu, Min-Hsuan, Elisabeth K. Gilbert, and Joyce E. Bono. "Is Beauty More Than Skin Deep? Attractiveness, Power, and Nonverbal Presence in Evaluations of Hirability." *Personnel Psychology* 75, no. 1 (2021): 119–146. https://doi.org/10.1111/peps.12469.

Worst-Online-Dater. "Tinder Experiments II: Guys, Unless You Are Really Hot You Are Probably Better off Not Wasting Your Time." *Medium*, October 2, 2014. https://medium.com/@worstonlinedater/tinder-experiments-ii-guys-unless-you-are-really-hot-you-are-probably-better-off-not-wasting-your-2ddf370a-6e9a.

Zielenziger, Michael. *Shutting Out the Sun: How Japan Created Its Own Lost Generation*. New York: Nan A. Talese, 2006.

www.ingramcontent.com/pod-product-compliance
Lightning Source LLC
Chambersburg PA
CBHW070556100426
42744CB00006B/295